'An unidentified bomber goes north'
by Observer T Bonar Lyon of No 33 Centre (Aberdeen) Royal Observer Corps at Nile Court, Ayr.
Published in the final double edition of *The Journal of the Royal Observer Corps Club* December 1942.

IMPERIAL WAR MUSEUM

FRIEND OR FOE

BEING
THE STORY OF
AIRCRAFT RECOGNITION

WRITTEN AND DESIGNED BY
TIM HAMILTON

HISTORICAL ADVISOR
CHARLES W. CAIN

LONDON: HMSO

© Text and book design copyright Tim Hamilton-Ayres, 1994.

First published HMSO 1994

ISBN 0 11 290496 3

HMSO publications are available from:

HMSO Publications Centre
(Mail, fax and telephone orders only)
PO Box 276, London, SW8 5DT
Telephone orders 071- 873 9090
General enquiries 071- 873 0011
(queuing system in operation for both numbers)
Fax orders 071- 873 8200

HMSO Bookshops
49 High Holborn, London, WCIV 6HB 071- 873 0011 Fax 071- 873 8200 (counter service only)
258 Broad Street, Birmingham, B1 2HE 021- 643 3740 Fax 021- 643 6510
33 Wine Street, Bristol, BS1 2BQ 0272- 264306 Fax O272- 294515
9- 21 Princess Street, Manchester, M60 8AS 061- 834 7201 Fax 061- 833 0634
16 Arthur Street, Belfast, BT1 4GD 0232 238451 Fax 0232 235401
71 Lothian Road, Edinburgh, EH3 9AZ 031- 228 4181 Fax 031- 229 2734

HMSO's Accredited Agents
(see Yellow Pages)
and through good booksellers

Printed in the United Kingdom for HMSO
Dd 0297401 C50 3/94

CONTENTS

ACKNOWLEDGMENTS

It is appropriate to express my sincere thanks to all those individuals and institutions whose records, personal remembrances and time created the backbone for this book. Orchestrated jointly by Charles W Cain and myself, the research work would not have been possible without the help of the following: First and foremost Sir Peter Masefield who was one of the leading lights in aircraft recognition during WW2 and who was kind enough to write the foreword to this book; Richard Riding and Michael Oakey of *Aeroplane Monthly* (direct descendant of *The Aeroplane*) for their help and permission to publish drawings, extracts and photographs that originally appeared in Temple Press publications; Leslie Whitfield for his immensely detailed memoirs and for much original material; Peter Endsleigh Castle for both his memories and for many of the line drawings in the book; Michael Cummings for his memories and for a new cartoon to end the final chapter; Derek Wood for a rare document; The Daily Telegraph for permission to reproduce Tony Holland's cartoon; and, in no particular order, Roger Freeman, Mike Hooks, James Oughton, Ron Moulton, Adrian Bishop, Dr Denys Voaden, Wacek Klepacki, John Pothecary, Ken Wakefield, Serge Blandin, Graham Mottram the Curator of the Fleet Air Arm Museum and the staff of the Public Record Office at Kew. On the editorial side I would like to thank Bill Ireson for his work on checking the final manuscript for errors of consistency and style. And for encouragement and enthusiasm, Bob Barnard of HMSO and Dr Christopher Dowling of the Imperial War Museum. Every publisher has a face and to me HMSO is Philip Brooks who listens to my ideas and helps forge them into print. Lastly, I have again to thank Charles W Cain for his unstinting efforts in every direction but with a particular mind to historical accuracy.

ANSWERS AND RECOGNITIONS

Wren Oddentifications: Front Cover - Miles Messenger as Montgomery. Page 120 - Il'yushin Il-4 bomber as Stalin. From *The Aeroplane* on page 82: Left - Dornier Do 17. Right - Bristol Blenheim 1. From the *Aircraft Recognition Journal* on pages 118 and 119: 'Cummings Railway Halt' - Tree reading from left to right, Marauder, 'Tony', Mustang. Tunnel, Ju 290. Signal, Corsair. Cow, 'Oscar'. Level crossing gate, Fw 190. Rear of rail coach, 'Val'. Bush, Do 217. Fortress, Typhoon. Luggage truck, B-29. Cyclist's legs, Hurricane. Water pool, Sunderland. 'Recognitos' - From left to right, Tomahawk, Zeke (Zero), Me 323, Vengeance, Wellington III. Chapter end piece targets : Page 9 - Bleriot XI. Page 37 - DH9A. Page 61 - Miles Hawk Tnr III. Page 91 - Spitfire 1. Page 121 - DH Mosquito IV. Page 137 - Airspeed Ambassador. And the Peter Endsleigh Castle drawing on page 37 an SE 5A.

DEDICATED TO

My mother, Observer Audrey Ayres,
a plotter at Headquarters No 9 Group
Royal Observer Corps in Yeovil, Somerset,
whose loving encouragement furthered a
growing interest in flying and aeroplanes.

and for
MICHÈLE and ALEXANDRA

FOREWORD

Throughout the history of warfare on land and at sea, a continuous and serious problem has been to distinguish friend from foe. Hence, since the earliest times, there came about the steady evolution of distinguishing marks in the form of badges, uniforms, flags and other markings in an endeavour to make clear who was who? Even so, military and naval records are littered with tragic stories of the results of mistaken identity. When aircraft added a wholly new element and new confusions to these tasks of recognition, there came a pressing need, not only from ground forces and ships at sea, as to when - and when not - to fire on aircraft, but also from pilots and observers in the air to know who was the enemy and who was not? From the start, there was, understandably, an urge to shoot first and to ask afterwards. A major saving grace was the considerable inaccuracy of anti-aircraft fire and that the chief invaders of British air space during the early part of the First World War were Zeppelin airships, not easily confused for anything else in the absence of all but a very few Allied counterparts.

Right from the start, there was some ambiguity, and even confusion, between the terms identification and recognition. Early work of an uneven quality during the First World War, and that produced right up to the start of the Second World War, went generally by the name of 'aircraft identification'. And that title was used, also, in our first series of publications from 'The Aeroplane' during 1939. Thereafter, the word 'aircraft recognition' was used, rather more accurately because of the emphasis upon 'seeing and believing', and it became the accepted term. Going back to first principles, the term 'recognition' is defined in the Oxford Dictionary as 'to know again', or, 'to perceive to be seen as previously known'. By contrast (and rather splitting hairs) 'to identify' has been defined as 'to ascertain to be the same, from previous knowledge'.

Between the Wars, the enjoyable subject of endeavouring to identify the rapidly multiplying types of aircraft was largely confined to those who, professionally or as spectators, visited air displays to watch and participate in the air races and other competitions. Officialdom had other preoccupations and the subject of aircraft recognition - its potential future importance little considered - was left to those imbued with the 'air-faring outlook' and the small numbers of the part-time members of the volunteer, civilian Observer Corps. When War came in September 1939, a wholly different situation brought a new urgency to the subject and, in spite of a number of tragic incidents from mistaken identity, little was done officially - and what was done, was both crude and inaccurate. The matter was brought to a timely head by the Guildford Post of that enthusiastic body of 'Dad's Watchers' in November 1939, when a meeting was arranged at the for a first assembly of a 'Hearkers Club' (so named because, in rural terms, they were 'out an 'earkin and watchin' by day and by night). Invited to this watershed meeting, as the then Technical Editor of *The Aeroplane*, to lecture on 'Aircraft and their recognition' it also marked the beginning of a profound personal involvement with the subject which was to continue for many years.

The history of my involvement is well detailed in the following pages. In this, I had the privilege of leading a splendid team, the principle names of whom are all mentioned. There are, however, those who directly and indirectly, ought also to be remembered in the intricate story of the drive towards distinguishing friend from foe. They were: C F Andrews of Vickers-Armstrongs, Col George Bijur of the US Army 8th Air Force, Sqn Ldr C H Blythe RAFVR at the Air Ministry, Leonard Bridgman of *All The World's Aircraft*, Peter Brooks of the Fleet Air Arm, Capt Donald Bulmer of the Directorate of Army Kinematography, Leslie Carr of *The Aeroplane*, Flt Lieut J G Gent RAFVR, Sqn Ldr H F King of Air Intelligence, E Colston Shepherd of *The Aeroplane*, Charles Sergeant of the Ministry of Home Security, Lieut Arthur Spencer RNVR, Charles Tapp of The Royal Observer Corps, Lieut A G Villiers RNVR and Gabrielle Welford of the *Inter-Services Journal of Aircraft Recognition*. One has to say of all of these people that at the time they received little recognition themselves, though their combined endeavours forged many bonds of interest and friendship, not only in aircraft recognition, but in promoting interest in aviation generally, which had a valuable spin-off influence on the revival of British aviation after the War.

Finally I would like to congratulate Tim Hamilton on the excellence of his work in compiling this unique book, the first ever to chronicle the story of aircraft recognition, aided by my old friend and former colleague, Charles Cain, the final editor of *The Aeroplane Spotter*. Clearly, an immense amount of research has gone into it to record in detail the history of a subject which from a shaky start during the First World War became one of the great combined operations of the Second World War - and which saved many lives and engendered so much enthusiasm.

Sir Peter G Masefield

MA CEng Hon DSc Hon DTech Hon FRAes

FORMATIVE YEARS

By the outbreak of the First World War in August 1914, Britain's military forces were preoccupied with the problems of mobilisation and strategic positioning in order to establish an advantageous front. Little or no thought had been given to the possibility of an aerial attack on Britain. As far as defence was concerned, there existed a traditional division of labour between the two Services; the Royal Navy being responsible for keeping the seas open and the Army for defending the Navy's shore establishments with coastal artillery or local garrisons. Thus, when the possibility of aerial attack was

considered, it was assumed that it would be in the form of bombardment by one of the German airships and that it would automatically become the Army's responsibility to deal with it. Furthermore, the International Hague Peace Convention of 1907, to which both Britain and Germany were signatories, had decreed that the 'Bombardment of undefended places by any means whatever was forbidden.' The Hague Convention did not take into account the possibility of aerial warfare and was imprecise in its definition of 'undefended places'; but it was with the terms of the Convention in mind that in

The initial threat, an Imperial German Navy Zeppelin of 1914/15 photographed over the North Sea.

Britain a whole host of important Government and military targets were deliberately left without any form of defence at all. The Royal Navy had, to some extent, allowed for this situation by positioning its seaplane bases to enable the flying of defensive patrols and by basing a Royal Naval Air Service (RNAS) squadron at Dunkerque with a policy of 'Vigorous and offensive attacks on the enemy's airsheds and aircraft before they reach these shores.' Further defensive patrols were mounted by the Army's Royal Flying Corps (RFC), but only with training aircraft; the main body of the force having already left to provide a reconnaissance role in France. Liaison between the Navy and the Army had never been good and the situation of defence from aerial attack was, in August 1914, without policy or command and *ad hoc* to the extreme. Aware of the danger Lord Kitchener, the newly appointed Secretary-of-State for War, requested that the Admiralty assume immediate responsibility for Air Defence until such time as the Army, which was busily recruiting to boost its manpower in France, possessed the trained personnel to take over. Mr Winston Churchill, then First Lord of the Admiralty, looking for an opportunity to heighten the profile of the Navy in what looked like being a predominantly land-based war, applied himself to creating a master plan for the defence of Britain against aerial attack. There was little point in changing that which worked, and so the Army's Royal Garrison

Artillery was left with its gun batteries to defend the naval ports; but in London the Navy undertook the new requirement for gun emplacements. The provision of aircraft for defensive patrols also became a naval responsibility, with the RFC contracted to assist once it fulfilled its commitment overseas.

Supported by a committee of experts (including Capt Murray Sueter, the Director of the Air Department of the Navy), Churchill next addressed himself to a detailed plan for the aerial defence of London. A proposal was put forward by Sueter that involved the creation of a defensive ring of guns, searchlights and observers, inside which would be contained all the principal Government and state buildings. Outside this, at a 10 mile radius, would be another ring inside which would be an even distribution of landing grounds where aircraft could be stationed. Existing aerodromes would be augmented by the creation of two new air stations in the east, at Joyce Green in Kent and Hainault Farm in Essex. Implementation of Sueter's proposal, included the provision of emergency landing sites in Regents Park, Battersea Park and Hyde Park as well as in the grounds of Buckingham Palace. The required personnel were found by creating an Anti-Aircraft Corps with suitable men drawn from the Royal Naval Volunteer Reserve (RNVR), and by observer volunteers being signed up as Special Constables who

A Taube (Dove) monoplane of the type used by the Imperial German Navy to drop the first bomb.

would perform duties in addition to their civilian occupations. Following a special request by its Lord Mayor, and as men and equipment became available, the central London defence ring was expanded to include the square mile of the City of London. To confuse the enemy's navigation by night all street lights were dimmed, with stretches of main road blacked out completely to eliminate easy map references. The parks, apparent from the air as black holes, were criss-crossed with dimmed lights to further confuse this picture. By October 1914 Churchill advised the War Cabinet that he did not believe an aerial attack could produce a decisive military result. But, considering the total lack of defences for London's residential areas, he warned that 'Loss and injury, followed by much public outcry will probably be incurred in the near future.'

Britain's defences sat and waited. An aerial attack by a Zeppelin now seemed certain. Aeroplanes, it was believed, didn't have the capability to carry both the fuel required and a significant bomb load. Therefore, no thought was given to basic aircraft identification which, if implemented, would have been confused by the number of German aircraft privately purchased before the war only to be impressed into RNAS service to aid home defence measures. By December, London's defences were in place and all that remained was to establish a system of alerting the control centre that the enemy was *en route*. The only body of men available for this duty was the police force, and all police personnel within a 60 mile radius of London were ordered to look out for airships. On sighting a Zeppelin they were commanded to telephone the phrase 'Anti Aircraft London' to the nearest exchange, which would connect them directly to the Admiralty control room.

When the first attack came, on 21st December, it was delivered, to everyone's surprise, by an unchallenged German Navy Taube monoplane which dropped two bombs into the sea off the Admiralty Pier at Dover. On Christmas Eve another German Navy Taube made history by dropping the first bomb on English soil. This landed in the garden of a house close to Dover Castle and records state that: 'A man who was cutting holly was blown out of a tree and a number of windows were broken.' The following day an Albatros seaplane flew up the Thames Estuary to be greeted by anti-aircraft guns, three RFC aeroplanes from Eastchurch on the Isle of Sheppey and three RNAS aeroplanes from the Isle of Grain. The intruder immediately turned back, dropping two bombs on Cliffe Fort before escaping out to sea. Then, on 19th January 1915, two German Navy Zeppelins reached the Norfolk coast. One dropped nine bombs on Great Yarmouth while the other dropped seven on King's Lynn, killing 2 people and injuring 13. The effect of these raids was to create confusion and indignation among the public. Militarily, the failure of the aeroplane raids and the relative success of the Zeppelins reinforced belief that the enemy would confine its use of aeroplanes, albeit carrying bombs, to a reconnaissance role. Some action was demanded and extra guns were positioned in London, an Eastern Mobile Air Defence Force was formed and work commenced on producing a warning poster. This advised members of the public to familiarise themselves with the appearance of different types of aircraft and to report any hostile types seen in country districts. At the same time the Admiralty issued a pamphlet containing the same information for use by its gun crews and the police observers. This material is significant only in that it marks the first efforts to promulgate aircraft identification. It must, however, have further added to the confusion with the untrained eyes of the public and the police reporting the majority of British training aeroplanes as hostile.

PUBLIC WARNING

The public are advised to familiarise themselves with the appearance of British and German Airships and Aeroplanes, so that they may not be alarmed by British aircraft, and may take shelter if German aircraft appear. **Should hostile aircraft be seen,** take shelter **immediately** in the nearest available house, preferably in the basement, and remain there until the aircraft have left the vicinity: do not stand about in crowds **and do not touch unexploded bombs.**

In the event of **HOSTILE** aircraft being seen in country districts, the nearest Naval, Military or Police Authorities should, if possible, be advised immediately by Telephone of the TIME OF APPEARANCE, the DIRECTION OF FLIGHT, **and whether the aircraft is an Airship or an Aeroplane.**

GERMAN | BRITISH

AIRSHIPS | AIRSHIPS

Note specially the shape of the Airships and the position of the passenger cars

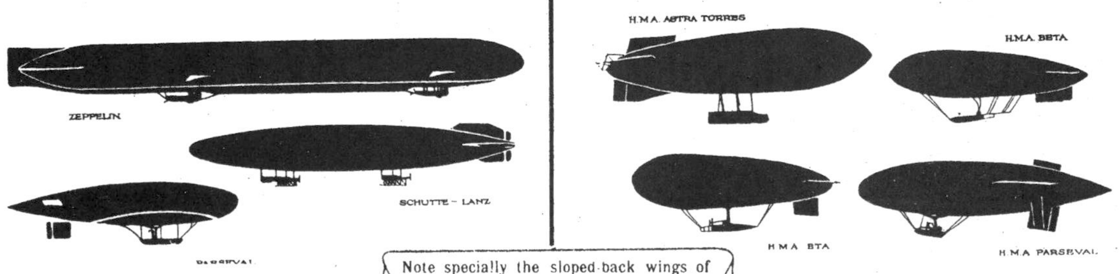

Note specially the sloped-back wings of the German Aeroplanes

AEROPLANES | AEROPLANES

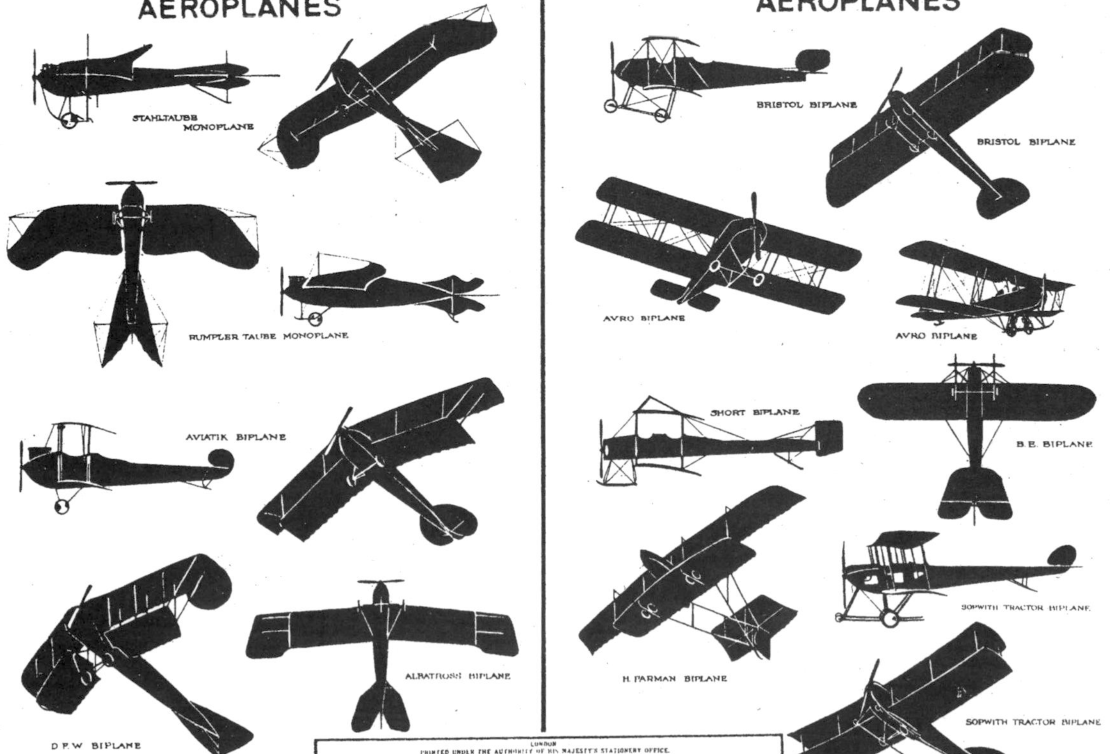

LONDON
PRINTED UNDER THE AUTHORITY OF HIS MAJESTY'S STATIONERY OFFICE.
By SIR JOSEPH CAUSTON & SONS, LIMITED, 9, Eastcheap, E.C.

To be purchased either directly or through any Bookseller, from WYMAN & SONS, LIMITED, 29, Breams Buildings, Fetter Lane, E.C., and 54, St Mary Street, Cardiff; or H.M. STATIONERY OFFICE (Scottish Branch), 23, Forth Street, Edinburgh; or E. PONSONBY, LIMITED, 116, Grafton Street, Dublin; or from the Agencies in the British Colonies and Dependencies, The United States of America, the Continent of Europe and Abroad of T. FISHER UNWIN, London, W.C.

PRICE TWOPENCE

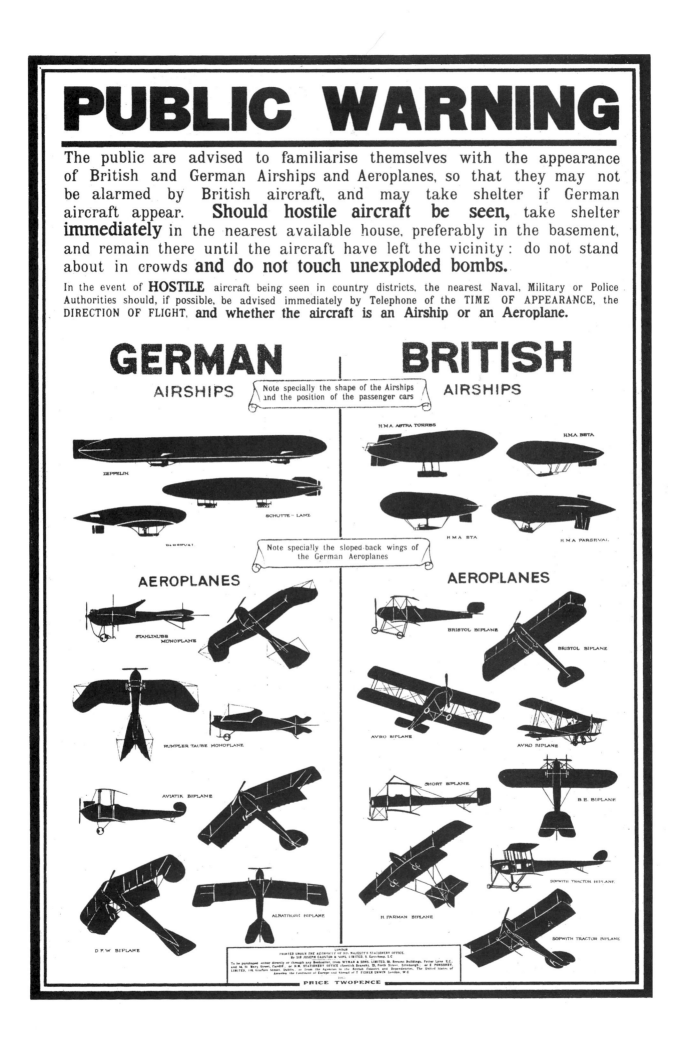

In France, General Galliéni, charged with the defence of Paris, took a less insular approach to the threat of aerial attack. Admittedly, Paris was much closer in range than London but France already had indulged in a long love affair with the aeroplane and General Joffre, the Chief of Staff, was quick to recognise both its potential and its threat. Assuming that hostile aeroplanes would fly at a height of 10,000 feet to keep above the ceiling of their anti-aircraft guns, the French military realised that visual identification by national marking or by appearance would be unreliable if not impossible. Therefore, they devised a system of plotting aircraft movements; suitably sited observers reported all movements and these reports were compared with all known other 'friendly' movements so isolating any intruders. To aid early detection, the French constructed mobile listening devices which greatly amplified the sound of approaching aircraft. These devices rotated and could therefore follow the sound, creating a 'plottable' track. Backed up

A complex, but effective, French revolving mobile aircraft sound locator used in the defence of Paris.

by mobile anti-aircraft guns and linked by telephone to a whole series of aerodromes, the French system benefited both from immediacy and the ability to be ready for attack from whatever direction it came. Identification of a particular aircraft was soon learnt as operators became familiar with the distinctive sounds of different aero-engines.

Britain's defences continued as planned, with extra guns distributed as they became available. A lull followed the first Zeppelin attack and, despite a spate of false alarms, no further aeroplane incursions were recorded. This vindicated the Admiralty's thinking and emphasis was placed on spotting enemy airships by night, with coastal searchlights as the mainstay of early warning. Flying at 11,000 feet, with an ability to switch off engines and drift silently on track, it was easy for the airships to make a surprise attack and it made them almost invisible at night. Despite this, no effort had yet been made to train RNAS and RFC pilots to fly night-time patrols. On 15th April 1915 a new series of Zeppelin attacks began, with indiscriminate bombing along the coasts of Norfolk and Suffolk and into Kent. The first raid on London took place on 31st May leaving behind 7 killed, 35 injured and a trail of damage. Public alarm was further heightened by the later raids of 17th August (9 killed, 48 injured), 7th September (18 killed, 38 injured) and 8th September (22 killed, 87 injured) which created damage estimated at half-a-million pounds, a large proportion of which was inside the central defence ring.

A major press outcry at what was happening pointed up the 'Terrible cost in lives and property' and editorial demands for instant action were accompanied by criticism of the Government: 'Something is seriously amiss when Zeppelins can sail in and out unhindered.' Within days of this anti Government campaign, the Admiralty announced the separation of the Defence of London from the overall Defence of Great Britain and placed it under the command of Admiral Sir Percy Scott, a gunnery expert. Scott was enamoured with aspects of the Paris defences, particularly the mobility of its units, and vowed that 'The defence of London by aircraft will begin over the Zeppelin sheds and the defence by gunfire at Britain's coast.' Despite a welcome reception for Scott's revised plan, both the War Cabinet and the Admiralty, in the belief that press criticism had been stifled, failed to supply the immediate resources needed for its success. And the eyes and ears of defence from aerial attack largely remained with the police as they went about their everyday business.

Brigadier-General Sir David Henderson, the Commander in Chief of the Royal Flying Corps in France (pictured here as a Major-General).

A British Squadron of French designed Morane Parasol scout monoplanes on the Western Front.

On the Western Front, which stretched from the Belgian coast to Switzerland, the RFC was involved in a very different type of war. When the first aircraft (of Squadrons 2, 3, 4 and 5) flew out to join the British Expeditionary Force (BEF) in France during 1914, their role was clearly defined. Under the command of Brig-Gen Sir David Henderson, they were designated as the 'Eyes of the Army' and greatly extended the reconnaissance information supplied by the balloon observers (who were winched up and down for artillery range spotting). Aeroplanes had the flexibility to sneak behind enemy lines and report back any activity with precise map references. Using 'Very' signals (some aircraft were equipped with primitive radio transmitters) they could report instantly on possible targets and then circle above to direct artillery fire. Although not primarily fighting aeroplanes (a role left to the RNAS with their long-range bombing sorties), they were exposed to enemy fire both from small arms and some anti-aircraft guns. To defend themselves they in turn carried small-arms weapons and trench bombs, which were little more than large grenades to be dropped over the side.

The French military air arm, together with exiled Belgian air units, flew alongside the RFC. Together they operated as a single force in much the same manner as their opponents of the Imperial German Air Service. In the early days of the war, there were comparatively few aeroplanes in relation to the extent of the front and, although Allied and enemy aeroplanes did fight each other in the air, the greatest threat came from the ground. 'Fired on by friend and foe alike', as Sir John French, the commander of the

BEF, acknowledged, the RFC found itself in a highly vulnerable position. The British infantry, unused to aeroplanes flying above them, mistook their comrades for the enemy and it was not until real disaster resulted from their enthusiasm that the French red, white and blue disc was adopted as an easily recognisable identification mark.

peculiar to the British, the General Headquarters Staff (GHQ) immediately ordered their own version of this sheet to be produced. Titled 'The Commoner Types of German Aircraft', it included seven aeroplanes and three airships all drawn in outline. A further irony was that the only source for the information required to produce

4th Division.

With reference to the revised diagrams of the more usual types of German aircraft sent you on 10th instant, I am directed to say that these diagrams can only be taken as a rough guide.

Certain of the allied types of aircraft resemble some of the German ones in general outline. Diagrams shewing the wing markings of Allied and German aeroplanes have recently been issued. These shew clearly the black Maltese Cross which is the distinctive mark of German aeroplanes.

No aeroplane is to be fired at by rifle fire unless the cross can be distinguished with certainty and rifle fire is not to be opened except by order of an officer.

G. F. Milne
B.G.G.S.

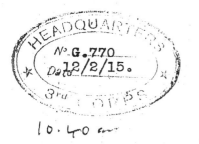

HEADQUARTERS
N°. G.770
Date 12/2/15.
3rd CORPS

10.40 am

The Germans, with the same motive of self-protection used the 'Iron Cross'. In addition, the French produced a sheet of four enemy aeroplane silhouettes and a drawing of a Zeppelin. Boldly lettered, albeit in French, 'FIRE ONLY AT THESE' the sheets were widely distributed among all the Allied troops to aid 'identification/recognition'. With a 'bloody mindedness'

the drawings was the Aero-Club de France, and the sheet was therefore issued under the guise of a 'Temporary measure pending a pamphlet on the subject.' That the pamphlet was not immediately forthcoming had as much to do with the increasingly rapid development of aeroplanes as with the course of the war and the lack of detailed information on enemy types.

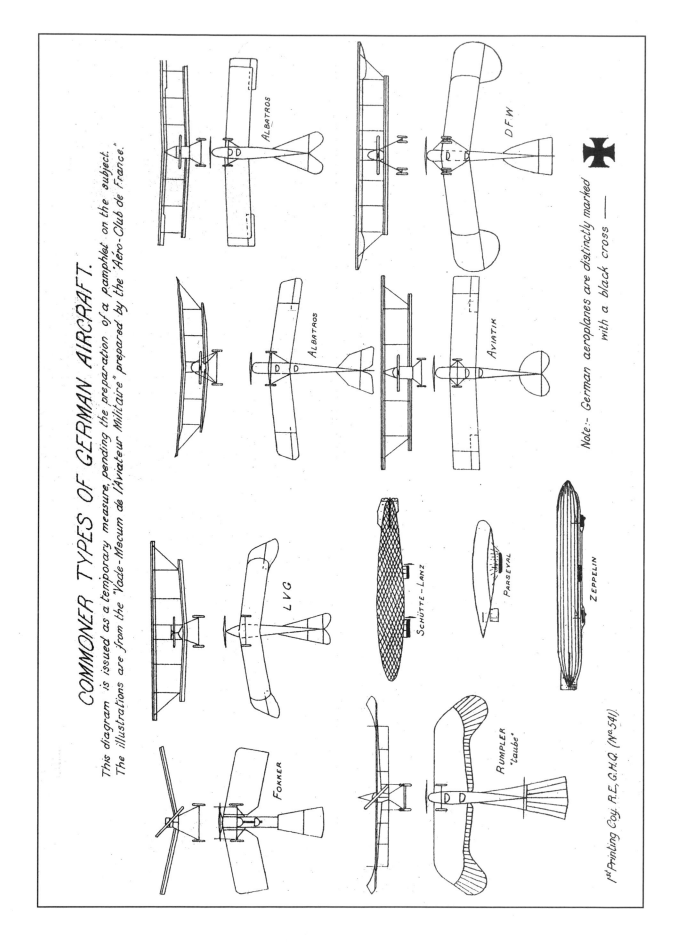

This simple sheet of line drawings was the first information on enemy aircraft ever issued by BEF GHQ in France and was circulated to all anti-aircraft units as well as to the RFC.

An artillery observation aeroplane (possibly German) on spotting duty flying over an intense artillery barrage somewhere along the Western Front, as photographed from the German side of the line.

The significance of the GHQ shcct of German aircraft types was considerable only in as much that its attempt at accuracy and specific purpose marked, much more than the well-known hostile aircraft poster, the true birth of British 'aircraft recognition' (although identification was still the word predominantly in use). This sheet, although not primarily designed for that purpose, was also distributed to pilots and observers of the RFC as their need became apparent. The RFC, however, with less than 100 serviceable aeroplanes, made their mark not only with the General Staff but also with the enemy. Often operating far behind the enemy's lines, the regular military intelligence gathered and the aerial photographs obtained by the pilots and observers enabled GHQ officers to make realistic tactical and strategic decisions. As the Imperial German Air Service began to achieve similar intelligence-gathering results from their side of the front, it became imperative for both opposing forces to eliminate as many of each others reconnaissance aeroplanes as possible. Initial attacks by patrolling flights of German aeroplanes soon led to the RFC sending up defensive patrols of its own and accompanying most single recon-

naissance aeroplanes with fully armed escorts.

Amid this dramatic escalation of aerial activity it was soon realised that accurate recognition, especially of friendly aircraft, was vital. Given the distance at which another aeroplane would be first noticed and in the short time available for decision making it was quite possible for one Allied patrol to find itself lining up for attack or taking evasive action from another Allied patrol. In addition to which, both the 'mêlée' of the moment and the brightness of the sky made it difficult, if not almost impossible, to distinguish national markings with any degree of accuracy. It therefore became vital to recognise enemy types and, although recognition was not a mandatory part of a pilot's or observer's training, there were severe military penalties for shooting up friendly aeroplanes. As yet no importance was given to distinguishing Allied aeroplanes from one another, let alone to recognising the enemy shapes by contrast. That such an idea could have confused the issue even further may have crossed the minds of Brig-Gen Sir David Henderson and his staff, since in early 1915 the RFC was flying every machine it could lay its hands on, including many French aeroplanes.

By the spring of 1915 RFC commanders finally accepted that a new era of aerial warfare had begun and officially permitted the mounting of Lewis machine-guns at the rear of the observer's cockpit in two-seat aeroplanes for both 'aggressive and defensive manoeuvres.' The Allies at that time had little reason to fear German aero-

planes because, although similar in performance and armament, the Germans were outnumbered by more than two to one. The greatest danger in the air came from the ever-increasing accuracy of the German anti-aircraft guns against which altitude was the only defence. These were nicknamed 'Archie' after the habit of British pilots addressing the shells bursting around them with a current music hall tag 'Archibald, certainly not!' Gunnery training was introduced for pilots

and observers, versions of which involved simple pole-mounted models being moved through the air at a scale speed while the trainee attempted to maintain it in a gunsight.

The next significant turn of events occurred on the 1st of April when the French pilot, Lieut Roland Garros, took off for a lone patrol in a Morane-Saulnier Parasol monoplane fitted with a forward-mounted Hotchkiss machine-gun which fired through the propeller. This was no sudden invention; the cam-driven interrupter gear which synchronised the firing had been the subject of much work by Saulnier in 1914. The mechanism had been perfected but the available Hotchkiss machine-gun fired at an uneven rate and the ammunition it used was also erratic in detonation. Tests had shown that one burst might fire cleanly through the revolving propeller, whilst a second burst could mistime and shoot-up the blades. With the new emphasis on aerial warfare now becoming apparent, Saulnier decided to try a deflector plate that could catch stray rounds and preserve the integrity of a wooden propeller. Initial tests proved that the idea worked and wedge-shaped deflectors with channels to direct the bullets were fitted to the new Type L monoplane that Lieut Garros flew. For nearly three weeks he became the scourge of the skies and German pilots were amazed by an aeroplane that flew straight at them and then opened fire. Unfortunately on 18th April, flying low behind enemy lines, Garros took a hit on his fuel line from ground fire. Gliding the Morane-Saulnier to a safe landing, he immediately set the aeroplane ablaze but to no real avail. The Germans were delighted to capture both Garros and the unburnt metal interrupter gear. They had an air-cooled Parabellum machine-gun with a more reliable timing on its rate of fire than the Hotchkiss, and set Anthony Fokker to develop a version of Saulnier's interrupter gear to be fitted to his latest high-performance monoplane. Fokker went one better and produced the 'E.1 Eindecker' fitted with his development of the interrupter gear which operated the forward-mounted Parabellum machine-gun but was fired by a trigger fitted to the control column. This meant that for the first time a pilot could totally concentrate on the complex flying manoeuvres required in aerial battles. Anthony Fokker's design met with the instant approval of the German chiefs of staff and the first E.1 Eindeckers reached the Western Front by mid-summer.

Forward-firing tractor aeroplanes brought with them a new dimension to the problems of identification 'friend or foe' - not least for the

SILHOUETTES D'AVIONS

DIAGRAMS OF AEROPLANES

The world's first recognition handbook produced by the French.

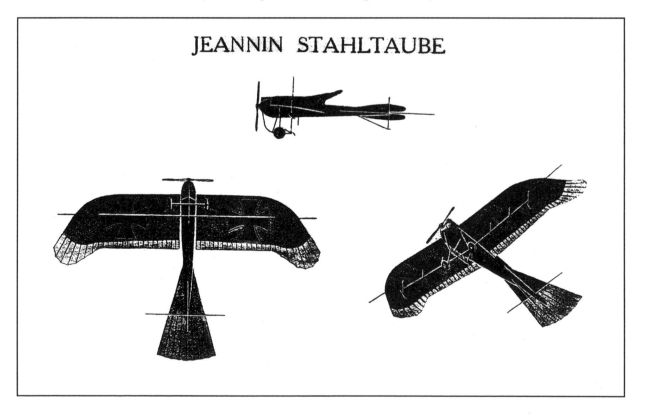

JEANNIN STAHLTAUBE

ground troops who were now subjected to low-level high-speed strafing runs. Fortunately the French, aided by the Aero-Club de France, seized the initiative from the British and published a recognition manual. Illustrated with three-position silhouettes of all the fighting aeroplanes to be encountered along the Western Front, it was written in both French and English and distributed to troops and airmen alike. Printed on a cardboard that would withstand use, and in a handy pocket size, it was accepted as the first of a series that never materialised. It did, however, precede the arrival of the Eindecker by a couple of months.

By the middle of 1915, Britain had adopted a similar system of plotting aircraft movements to that devised for the defence of Paris. This system was continually revised until it was thought that all aspects of air movement were adequately covered. In addition to the police, all coastguard stations and look-outs, and all ships patrolling both the North Sea and the English Channel were required to report aircraft sightings. This information was added to observations made by both Navy and Army gun and searchlight emplacements, and supplemented by reports of aircraft movements, both actual and intended, received via Military Intelligence from agents on the Continent. Individual air stations reported all movements of their own aircraft and further reports of movements of military machines were passed on by the War Office. All of this gathered data was marked on specially prepared charts in the Information Bureau of the Anti-Aircraft section of the Admiralty, to be investigated and passed, whenever necessary, to the defence stations concerned. Its purpose, in the words of an official communiqué, was 'to be possible, on a machine being sighted in any part of the country,

to tell immediately whether she is friendly or hostile.' On paper this looked good but in practice, although there were supposed to be direct lines of communication, a raiding aeroplane could have done its damage and been halfway home before the position of its initial sighting was passed to a suitable defence station. But, since the year 1915 produced only four single aeroplane raids on Britain (which were considered at the time as only of nuisance value) the main worry was enemy airships. These, of course, were much slower and on a clear day could be easily recognised at 10,000 feet. The need, therefore, was for more aeroplanes to locate and attack the airships and it was with this demand that Sir Percy Scott found himself playing into the hands of the Army. It had always been agreed that the Admiralty's control of the Defence of Britain was only an interim measure to overcome the lack of manpower. The RFC quite reasonably argued that if more machines were to be made available then they, not the RNAS, should have them. Lord Kitchener's Chiefs of Staff agreed that perhaps the time was right for the Army to step in and a six-month

A rare photograph of the Aircraft movement plotting room in London's Admiralty Headquarters.

The advent of the long-range bombing threat, an Imperial German Air Service two-seat LVG of 1916.

programme was put into operation for the transfer of Britain's defences to War Office control.

On 12th February 1916, amid a renewed offensive by the enemy who had been quiet since October 1915, the Admiralty stood down. The Defence of London, still being treated as a separate issue, was transferred four days later with a diffuse command structure involving seven 'fire' commands, a London commander for administration, GHQ Home Forces for training and operations, and aeroplane defences under the separate control of the RFC. Night-flying skills were to be the principle focus of attention and a devastating German airship attack on Liverpool during the night of 31st January, just prior to the transfer of control, reinforced the urgency. Some 22 sorties were flown by 18 aeroplanes against the raiders but to no effect. Despite flying within reach of several gun batteries, the enemy airships returned home unscathed having successfully deposited their fatal loads. The fact that Britain's defences failed to shoot down a single airship was not lost on the press, much to the Government's embarrassment. The furore and political debate that followed, however, obscured an important point: that all the other raids in the new offensive were made by single aeroplanes. Admittedly, they were merely on coastal targets but, unbeknown to the British, the Germans had already accepted that the airship was vulnerable; and it was with fast-moving and difficult-to-spot, aeroplanes that their future bombing initiatives would be made.

The first six months of War Office control did little to bolster confidence, achieving just one airship severely damaged by anti-aircraft fire and one seaplane downed by an RNAS fighter. Aeroplanes remained the country's prime defenders and GHQ Home Forces proposed increasing the number of squadrons available,

despite the priority demands for machines on the Western Front. The Admiralty, in opposition to the Army, made known its pessimistic views about night flying, otherwise little changed from the pattern of defence that was already established. Spring 1916 brought a temporary halt to the German raids and the War Cabinet seized the opportunity to aid the Army in France by reducing the planned home defence squadrons to eight.

The end of July saw the return of the Zeppelin raids on a regular basis but it wasn't until the night of 2nd/3rd September that the War Office scored its first real victory. Armed with specially developed incendiary ammunition, Lieut William Leefe Robinson of No 39 Squadron RFC, successfully brought down an airship in flames. In this instance he was aided by intense anti-aircraft fire but the technique learned led to a series of successes in which four Zeppelins were shot down by aeroplanes and a damaged fifth was finally claimed by an anti-aircraft gun crew. Disruption to the enemy raids was fundamental, scattering airships in all directions and considerably reducing their bombing effect. The greatest night for Britain's Home Forces came on the 27/28th November when 2 out of 10 Zeppelins were shot down and the raid routed. In the euphoria of belief that the Zeppelin menace had now been defeated, little attention was paid the following morning to the arrival of a single LVG aeroplane raider over London. This was the first time that an enemy aeroplane had attacked beyond the coastal towns; C G Grey, the redoubtable editor of Britain's leading aeronautical weekly *The Aeroplane*, only too well aware of the inadequacy of Britain's defences, was quick to pick up his pen: 'When the aeroplane raids start, and prove more damaging than the airship raids, the authorities cannot say that they have not had a fair warning of what to expect.'

The New German Giant

that is threatening Britain's shores.

Imperial German Air Service twin-engine Gotha.

By January 1917, amid a sense of self-congratulation that the measure of the Zeppelin had been met, a reduction in anti-aircraft defences was proposed. The Admiralty, now with little interest in home defence, insisted that gun production be immediately transferred to work for arming the merchant fleet against attacks by U-boats. The War Cabinet, ignoring both its own intelligence reports and C G Grey's prophetic warning, agreed and additionally ordered that two of the RFC's home defence squadrons be sent to France. Absence of any damaging large-scale raids during the first five months seemed to justify the War Cabinet's decisions, but the events of 25th May soon caused them to change their minds. At 5pm on the eve of the Whit Weekend, a force of 21 twin-engine Gotha bombers crossed the east coast and headed for London. Diverted by heavy cloud, they turned south and dropped their bombs on Folkestone, killing 95 people and leaving 195 injured. Free from any form of interception, the Gothas returned over the Channel to meet their only opposition from RNAS fighters based at Dunkerque. This first real aeroplane raid created chaos in the complacent minds of GHQ Home Forces - and the press, once the details were released, launched yet another attack on the Government. *The Times,* in an editorial on 28th May, suggested that the Home Defence squadrons had taken off too late because of 'Obvious shortcomings in the intelligence, observer and warning organisations.' Discussions on how to rectify this were

still taking place on 13th June when, in broad daylight, a diamond formation of 14 Gothas flew up the Thames and bombed the docks and areas around the City. Some 72 bombs were dropped on Liverpool Street Station and a school in Poplar received a direct hit killing 18 children - in total 162 people were killed and 432 injured. The Home Defence squadrons, with 92 aeroplanes in the air, reported that few of its pilots were even able to see the enemy, let alone get close enough to come within firing range. With the country in uproar, plans were laid to increase the strength of the RFC and adjustments were made to anti-aircraft gun positions reinforcing cover on the eastern side of London. Barely were these measures complete when the Gothas returned on 7th July bombing the East End and the City, again in broad daylight. The effect, or rather non-effect, of the defences was disastrous as before - the enemy losing only one of 21 Gothas to a coastal-based fighter as the formation made its way home.

Public outrage at the incompetence of the Home Defence Forces was at its greatest since the war began. The War Cabinet responded by demanding the return of two RFC squadrons from France but, with varying fortunes overseas, Earl Haig reluctantly returned one and finally diverted a squadron in training for the Western Front. The next move was to form a committee, and fortunately the lateral thinking Lieut-Gen J Smuts was made its chairman. He realised the inadequacy of simple defensive ground fire and understood the strength of the enemy's formation strategy. He also recognised the need for speed both in the reporting of enemy aeroplane sightings and in the response time to position RFC fighters in the correct sector ahead of the enemy. His solution was to fire giant barrages of shells into the path of the bomber formations, thus breaking them up and allowing small groups of RFC fighters to pick off lone individuals. To implement these ideas, a new London Air Defence Area (LADA) was created, commanded by Brig-Gen E B 'Splash' Ashmore. Called back from the BEF in France, Ashmore, who had alternated between the RFC and the Royal Artillery, applied his knowledge of utilising aeroplanes backed by his experiences of war at the front. His first move was to set up a line of guns as a barrier 20 miles to the east of London and (with Lieut-Col Simon) to establish a ring of artillery on a 25 mile radius of the centre, which would disperse the enemy formations. Three new RFC squadrons were formed and a number of wireless-equipped aeroplanes were designated for 'observation duties' to keep track of any invaders and to report their positions, altitudes and headings. The results were dramatic and immediate. On 12th August a formation of nine Gothas was met by a squadron of fighters and fled jettisoning its bombs *en route*. Then, on 22nd August, a formation of 10 (out of 15) Gothas crossed the eastern coastline to be met by the full force of the new defences. Three were shot down and the rest fled, jettisoning their bombs, only to be chased by various squadrons all the way to Belgium. The increased strength of Britain's defences now meant that any invading aeroplanes would have to fly, with their

Major-General E B 'Splash' Ashmore with his proposals for the specially positioned barrages of anti-aircraft fire, force raiding aeroplanes to turn into a trap or to climb above an accurate bombing range.

Anti-aircraft gun position in the heart of London.

On the night of 3rd September the Germans came back and, although spotted over the coast near Dover, four Gothas managed to reach the naval barracks at Chatham to drop their bombs, killing 130 ratings and injuring nearly the same number. The following night a formation of 10 Gothas bombed London and 16 more attacked targets in the south-east. Although ground fire was intense, only one Gotha was shot down and the night-flying fighter squadrons sent up failed to locate the enemy. Anticipating further press criticism, the War Cabinet called for a report from Smuts who, lacking any better idea than 'Attack is the best form of defence', suggested the possibility of erecting a balloon barrage carrying an apron of steel wire to force invading aeroplanes to a height where accuracy in bombing would be impossible. Ashmore implemented the idea and simplified it to just three or five balloons per apron, strung together with a horizontal wire from which vertical wires were suspended to form an aerial barrier. Twenty aprons were suggested but only two were installed along a line running from Tottenham across to Lewisham. Additionally, Ashmore worked out a new system for barrage fire that divided London into a series of squares. In these sectors, different patterns of barrage fire were arranged which would produce a curtain of shell bursts in a band width of 2,500 feet, set at varying heights. With the gun sites connected by telephone to a central command, enemy raiders

bomb loads, over a height of 10,000 feet and under cover of darkness. There were those who scoffed at the possibility but Ashmore believed it inevitable and, accepting that he had merely won a breathing space, continued to refine the defences.

A postcard of 1917 - 'Onlookers watch, as a downed Gotha G.IV bomber is examined by the military'.

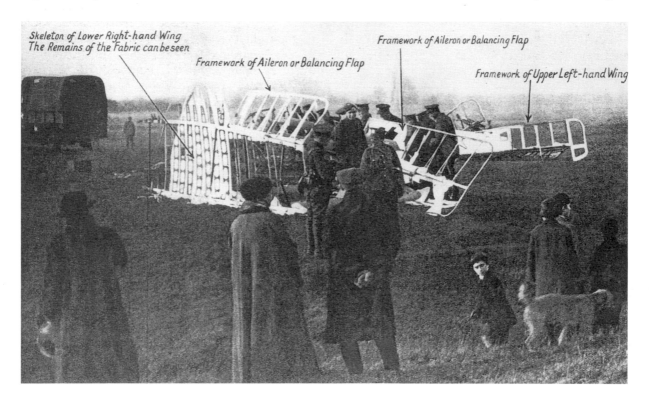

A loose formation of Gothas photographed on their way back to the Continent after a raid on London.

could be drawn into a trap and forced to climb or turn back. These sectors were out of bounds to all aircraft, and anything seen flying in them was to be declared hostile and immediately fired at. Further refinements of height observation and control were devised and added to Ashmore's system, aspects of which upset the War Office. At one point his orders were in danger of being overruled, particularly with the installation of direct telephone lines, until Sir John French intervened and Ashmore was given the freedom to continue.

During the autumn the defences were not seriously tested by the enemy, except for one abortive Zeppelin raid in which it was decided not to switch on searchlights or take any action that would reveal the new defence positions. However, in early December a new threat presented itself from across the Channel. This was the so-called 'Giant Gotha', a four-engine bomber well braced with protective machine-guns, and with a payload of some 4,500 lb. Its first appearance was made by a solo aeroplane during the night of 5/6th, followed at 2am by a formation of 15 conventional Gothas. The defences held fast and as well as bringing down three of the enemy aeroplanes, the barrage fire turned the formation away from London. But, on 18th December, a 'Giant Gotha' accompanied by six twin-engine raiders reached London and

bombed successfully, with the loss of only one machine as they returned over the coast.

Ashmore carefully analysed the situation. His equipment for defence was as good as it was ever going to be. Its deployment, however, was less than satisfactory and the success rate of the night fighters was particularly poor. What was required was a system of wireless contact with all the fighters so they could be dispatched to the exact position required, regardless of whether or not they made visual contact with the enemy. What was also required was a more sophisticated system of observation and reporting so that the enemy could be identified and accurately plotted, minute by minute, from the moment he was first sighted approaching the coast. This information could then be filtered through to a central command which would direct both guns and fighters, thus controlling the enemy's path as well as greatly increasing the chances of destroying him. Having convinced Lord French and General Smuts that this was the correct path to take, Ashmore began laying the groundwork for a formalised Observation Service which he knew would take several months to establish and become operational. Meanwhile he had to content himself with fine-tuning the existing defences, while brushing aside any criticisms that might be levelled as the result of a successful enemy attack.

An RFC montage picture, for propaganda use, of a defensive action high in the skies over France.

Aeroplanes, despite an initial abhorrence by the traditionalists among the Army's Chiefs of Staff, were playing a role of ever-increasing importance on the Western Front. By late 1915 the significance of accurate aerial observation and intelligence had led both the Germans and the Allies to realise that control of the skies meant control of the war. Greater effort was therefore put into designing fighters that could outpace the opposition, not only in firepower but also in performance. The arrival of the two-seat Bristol Fighter in mid-1917 at last gave the Allies an upper hand; it had the speed, manoeuvrability and the fixed forward-firing machine-gun of a small single-seat fighter and an observer's cockpit fitted with a 180 degree panning Lewis gun. Actions that were once waged on open battlefields by mounted divisions were now being fought at up to 16,000 feet between opposing squadrons of aeroplanes. While the war in the trenches continued as ever, a new war, fought for its own sake was being waged overhead by the 'Cavalries of the Clouds'. The ramification of this was not lost on the War Cabinet. Nor on

Smuts, who, in addition to his report on home defence, fulfilled a brief to report on 'Air Organisation' which resulted in a proposal for the RNAS and the RFC to be merged into a single independent air service. The architect of much of this proposal was Maj-Gen Henderson who returned from France in 1916 to become Director-General of Military Aeronautics (a thankless position as long as the Admiralty and the Army remained in opposition to each other). Recommendation for a separate service was reinforced by encouraging reports of the RFC in France and, like the home defence proposals, met with little opposition. By November 1917 the Royal assent was given to the Air Force (Constitution) Bill, officially creating the Royal Air Force (RAF) as a third fighting service.

As yet uninvolved in the Air Force politics at home, Maj-Gen Hugh Trenchard, who commanded the RFC in France, realised the need for numbers, as well as firepower and performance. In November 1917, impressed with the results achieved by the Bristol Fighter, he placed an order for over 1,000 to be delivered to France as they rolled out of production. Meanwhile numbers had to be achieved by multiple squadrons of mixed aeroplane types, with 'sweeps' comprising both RFC and other Allied air forces. This resulted in a curious mixture of British and French machines painted in various national military identification markings. To add to this confusion, the United States entered the war, and in August 1917 dispatched to France the 1st Aero Squadron of the American Expeditionary Force (AEF). Admittedly the American pilots were not yet to fly into combat and were equipped with French aeroplanes, but

could only be recognised by shape and therefore type, and that shape was very often presented at fast closing-speeds and at an oblique back-lit angle. The French had already gone some way to addressing the problem by updating their original book of 'silhouettes' with a series of actual silhouette cards showing various angles. These were published in the spring of 1917, in both English and French editions, and continually updated as new aeroplanes or versions found their way to the front. Ostensibly designed for use by Allied ground forces, as a defensive measure to prevent being casualties from 'friendly' fire, they were nevertheless issued to all Allied

MORANE MONOCOQUE
French single-seater tractor monoplane.

A.P.⋕S.S.
Process Section

G 13 Avril 1917.

One of a series of French silhouette cards.

they brought with them yet another paint scheme and a further variation on three-colour identification roundels. In the 'mêlée' that inevitably resulted from an engagement with the enemy, aircraft identification and recognition was becoming as difficult and confusing for the pilots as it was for those manning the anti-aircraft guns. Accepting that it was both impossible and dangerous for aeroplanes to get close enough in the air to identify correctly national markings before opening fire, the time had come to treat aircraft recognition seriously. Aeroplanes

pilots although there was still no mandatory obligation to do so.

By 1918 the problem that angered the French was not so much the stray bullets from the ground but the stream of incidents in which their aeroplanes were shot at by other Allied pilots, with consequent loss of both machines and lives. Complaints were made to Maj-Gen John Salmond, the new commander of the RFC in France. (Trenchard had returned home to become Chief of the Air Staff and help with the

9B/446G. 1528

HEADQUARTERS
51ST
WING R.F.C.
No. C/57W/G.4.
DATE 11-5-18

9th Wing, R.A.F.
51st Wing, R.A.F. ✓

1.   Several cases have occurred lately of our machines
attacking French machines.   Three French machines have
been brought down, in two cases with fatal results.   In
each instance the French machine was attacked well our
side of the line.   Although, of course, it is
essential to investigate any machine, not clearly
recognised as one of our own, whereever seen there is
no excuse for attacking allied machines especially on
our side of the lines, where there is always time to
make absolutely certain whether a machine is hostile
or allied.   All French machines are clearly marked and
with reasonable care no mistake should occur.   The
Breguets, which somewhat resemble German machines, have
specially large circles in order to distinguish them
more clearly.

2.   The 10th French Army Aviation Headquarters at BEAUVAL
are arranging to send machines of each type to Fighter
Squadron aerodromes in your Wing, so that pilots and
observers may study their appearance both on the ground
and in the air.   The dates and times at which these
machines will fly over your Aerodromes will be notified
to you in due course.   You will ensure that as many
pilots and observers as possible are on the aerodrome
to take note of the peculiarities of each type.   Some
machines should be in the air and note the appearance
of the French machines from different points of view.
The peculiarities and best means of recognition of
each type must be clearly noted and impressed on all
concerned.

Brigadier-General,
Commanding 9th Brigade,
Royal Air Force.

In the Field,
11th May 1918.

P/

30

The pilots of a French squadron of Nieuport 17.C scouts debrief after a sortie across the German lines.

inauguration of the RAF.) Directives were issued to squadron commanders in the field but to no immediate avail. Memoranda travelled from GHQ to HQ Brigades and from Brigades to HQ Wings. Salmond ordered: 'Will you please take steps to ensure that every officer is instructed in the main features of construction which will enable them to distinguish Allied from Enemy machines in the air.' And: 'Squadron Commanders will make it their personal responsibility to circulate diagrams and silhouettes of Allied and Enemy machines which are issued from time to time by G.H.Q. to all pilots at present with or newly posted to the Squadron.' Shortly after the foundation of the RAF, on the 1st of April 1918, matters came to a head and the attention of all its pilots was drawn to the urgent necessity of establishing the identity of supposed enemy machines before moving into the attack: 'Cases of our own and Allied machines being attacked by pilots of the R.A.F. are of far too frequent occurrence. While making every allowance for the heat of the moment and the necessity of obtaining the initiative in the attack, it cannot but reflect grave and culpable carelessness on the part of any pilot responsible for the attack of an Allied machine.' This was followed on 11th May by a directive from Maj-Gen Salmond: 'Further to my C.R.A.F. of the 5th

May, yet another case has occurred of a French machine being shot down by a British aeroplane. Two other similar cases have occurred in the last four days. Their recurrence is having a serious effect on the previous good relations between the French and British flying services. Silhouettes or photographs of all French machines with the exception of the Salmson will at once be placed on the wall of a hut to which all pilots must have continuous access. All pilots will be ordered to study them. A recurrence of such incidents will be followed by severe disciplinary action being taken on the pilot or pilots concerned.'

The need for a proper recognition manual had never been more clearly defined and was already in preparation, being organised by GHQ France for the newly created Air Ministry in London. Based on material supplied by the various Allied aircraft manufacturers and from intelligence sources and captured examples where enemy aircraft were concerned, it was planned to be a definitive work on the subject. The trouble was that it wasn't going to be available for several months. The French, however, well aware that the existing information didn't seem to be getting through to the pilots, came up with a practical and immediate solution - a 'Flying Circus' of French machines. This proposition came at

First to be published was the 'Types of British Aeroplanes' (in May 1918), rapidly followed by the German Aeroplane volume above .

the same time that Salmond was issuing his directive and was originally only supposed to be a flypast for the purpose of recognition but, with the French flair for showmanship, it soon turned when it became the RAF's turn to familiarise the French with British machines and he was detailed to fly an SE5A. The French squadron that he visited was called the 'Storks' and flew Spads, its leader was the famous French ace, Guynemer: 'A race was held between the two special Spads and the SE5. Their speeds were almost identical, but the high compression Spad climbed quicker. After the race was over, Guynemer and I held a demonstration combat over the aerodrome.' It was with such reciprocal activities that both camaraderie and recognition skills were repaired and the subsequent reduction of incidents of 'own goals' proved that the 'Flying Circus' worked.

 As June turned into July the British recognition manuals became available and consisted of booklets devoted to national types of aeroplanes. They were, almost with a sense of one-upmanship, far superior to the French publications and devoted a double page to each aeroplane. The right-hand page comprised either three clear photographs, or drawings of near photographic quality, while the left depicted five silhouette angles and a detailed technical description with dimension and performance data. Issued by the Air Council as Field Service publications, they undoubtedly proved interesting reading for Allied pilots. Whether they were the ideal aid to recognition is questionable but they followed the precedent for photographic-style presentation that was being set by the leading periodicals of the day.

An RFC squadron of RE.8s lined-up in readiness on an airfield near the Western Front in 1918.

FOKKER TRIPLANE (Type D.R.i.).

9

A typical page from the newly formed Air Ministry's July 1918 Field Service Publication (F.S.47.)
Types of German Aeroplanes.

PLATE 1.

A private circulation booklet produced in early 1919 to celebrate the work of
The Metropolitan Observation Service.

PLATE 2.

The late summer of 1918 saw Ashmore's LADA home defence scheme firmly in place and working. All military units in the Command (guns, searchlights, balloons, aerodromes), the existing police forces and coastguards were all part of the new observation network. Additional cover in previously open stretches was provided by special observation posts manned by either volunteer police specials or medically downgraded soldiers. Each observation post was linked by permanently connected direct telephone line to one of 25 sub-control centres. Each of these centres would receive information from its group of observers and plot reports of sightings or sounds of aircraft movements directly onto a large-scale map. A number of plotters would identify each initial report with an identifying marker which would then be moved to correspond with updated information as it was passed from one or more observation points who were following that particular aircraft movement. Raised above the plotters with an overall view of sector activity were tellers, who were in direct and constant telephone link with LADA Control Centre, passing filtered information on the overall movements depicted in front of them. LADA Control Centre duplicated the set-up at the sub-controls but on a much broader scale with a map table containing each of the 25 sectors. The plotters there received their information directly from the various sub-control tellers, positioning markers to plot the progress of aircraft movements within the whole LADA area. Emphasis was placed on the exact time of reports and a dominating clock had its face divided into colour segments so that when a report was updated the marker on the map would be changed to correspond with the colour segment into which the minute hand just moved. This had the advantage of being able to tell at a glance how old the report was and therefore to interpret its accuracy or reliability.

A gallery was positioned overlooking the map table at which sat Maj-Gen Ashmore with officers controlling gun sites, balloons, fighter aeroplanes, the police and fire services. Warnings could now be given directly to the areas concerned with an estimated time of a possible attack by raiders. Likewise, guns could be orchestrated to form a trap with some deliberately kept silent and others activated to force enemy formations to split up or move in the direction that suited LADA. Moreover, the officer in charge of fighter aeroplanes was linked by telephone line directly to a powerful wireless transmitter, situated at Biggin Hill in Kent, through which constantly updated instructions could be passed to the wireless-equipped flight commanders in the air. Initially there were problems but, with the addition of short-wave transmitters in the flight commanders' aircraft tuned to receivers in every fighter, instructions from LADA Control Centre could be turned into practical defence tactics within minutes of first

Drawings showing an Observation Service sub-control centre with a plotter at work.

being transmitted. A series of exercises soon ironed out any wrinkles in the observation and reporting systems and constant practise increased both speed and accuracy. All Ashmore needed was for the enemy to launch a raid for his LADA scheme to be properly tested.

In August 1918 there was a significant change of emphasis on the Western Front as the Allies scored victory after victory, pushing the front steadily north. Long-range damage was now being inflicted by bombers flying deep into Germany under the command of Trenchard's 'Independent Air Force'. (Maj-Gen Trenchard resigned as Chief of the Air Staff following disagreement with Lord Rothermere the new Secretary-of-State for Air. Rothermere, under political pressure, also resigned and was replaced by Sir William Weir, with Maj-Gen Sykes as Chief of the Air Staff. Trenchard, being too valuable to lose, was allowed to create an independent bombing force with its own direct access to the Air Council.) After the stalemate situation of the two previous years, Allied morale lifted, although it was still felt that the war would not be over until spring 1919 when

the Americans promised there would be a huge influx of their troops. Aircraft recognition was now firmly established as a necessity for both those in the air and those on the ground. Even so, nothing was done about formalised teaching of the subject and RAF pilots and observers, who had the greatest need because of the speed at which the decision 'friend or foe' was made, were still left to their own devices with the threat of severe disciplinary action if they got it wrong. At home, Ashmore's force, 'The Metropolitan Observer Service', was now seen as an integral part of home defence. Although still unproven in action (the last German bomber raid was four months earlier in May 1918), it had already demonstrated its potential through the ongoing series of exercises, some of which were observed by other senior military commanders. Here the decision 'friend or foe' was left out of the equation for the observers themselves. Despite the issue of binoculars to all observation posts, the requirement was merely to report aircraft movements without need to recognise specific aeroplanes. The identification of raiders or friendly aeroplanes was made at the sub-controls and ultimately at LADA Control Centre, based on

HM King George V, with his staff officers, visits an RAF field headquarters in France during 1918.

known aeroplane movements in the sectors much as had been the case in 1915.

On 3rd November 1918 Austria signed a peace with the Allies, but it still came as a surprise when six days later the Germans requested safe conduct for a mission to discuss an Armistice. Germany had crumbled from within under the pressure of near revolution by many of its people. After four years of continual fighting in Europe, the War Cabinet and the newly formed Air Ministry and RAF could stand back and look at what they had achieved, which was considerable especially in the latter years. However, with the signing of the Armistice on 11th November, the problems were now reversed. It was not so much a question of developing and refining, as what to do with the thousands of pilots, aeroplanes and a Metropolitan Observer Service that was no longer needed.

**'The birth of the Royal Air Force,
with its wonderful expansion and development,
will ever remain one of the most
remarkable achievements of the Great War.'**

AIRMINDEDNESS

With the war behind them, members of the Air Council now had to look to the future with a form of transport that was barely a dozen years old. Their first task was to examine the report of the Civil Aerial Transport Committee (formed in 1917 in anticipation of the peace). The fundamental recommendation of the Committee was that the Air Ministry should assume control of aviation activities both civil and military. The report was accepted in principle and, in February 1919, a newly-combined War and Air Ministry (with Winston Churchill replacing Weir as Secretary-of-State) returned Trenchard to Chief of the Air Staff, RAF, and moved Sykes sideways under the title of Controller-General, Civil Aviation. From their respective points of view both Trenchard and Sykes were required to produce memoranda on the future of aviation. Trenchard stated the case for a permanent Air Force which should be built and developed in its own right and be available as a tactical arm to the Navy or Army when needed. Sykes, in his new position, reiterated the Imperial ideas for aviation that he had embraced while still Chief of the Air Staff. He wrote in depth on the possibilities of establishing long-distance passenger routes both to link the outposts of the British Empire and to foster regular trade with countries halfway round the world. To this end he roundly praised the *Daily Mail* £10,000 prize, still 'on offer' from 1913, for the first non-stop trans-Atlantic flight. Trenchard, too, saw the sense in such a challenge since it would not only boost the image of the RAF but also would demonstrate to other powers that, if required, aerial reinforcements could be brought quickly from North America. He had also been impressed by a world altitude record of 30,500 feet established on 2nd January 1919 by a DH9, flown by Capt A Lang with observer Lieut A Blowes from the experimental aircraft establishment at Martlesham Heath in Suffolk. The achievement of these RAF officers and their aircraft had captured the interest of the press and the imagination of the public. It was through the politics of portraying the RAF at the forefront of aviation that Trenchard knew his future support would come.

The trans-Atlantic prize aroused much interest from aircraft and engine manufacturers. Aircraft built by Sopwith, Martinsyde, Handley Page and Vickers, all powered by Rolls-Royce engines, looked to be the main contenders. Harry Hawker, test pilot for the Sopwith Aviation Company and Lieut-Cdr Mackenzie-Grieve of the Royal Navy, were the first to establish themselves at St John's, Newfoundland in March 1919 for a west to east crossing. While they waited for suitable weather the Martinsyde team of F P Raynham and Capt C W F Morgan arrived with the clear intention of beating Hawker to it. Capt John Alcock and Lieut Arthur

Whitten Brown, both RAF retired, were running some weeks behind with their planned attempt in a considerably modified Vickers Vimy bomber. The Americans, too, were planning a crossing with three Curtiss NC flying-boats, albeit with stops (which put them out of the competition) and by a southerly route via the Azores to Lisbon. Other contenders were in various stages of preparation, one proposing the more difficult east to west route. Although press attention was firmly focused on Newfoundland, the Australian Government chose this moment to announce another prize, of £A10,000, for the first aeroplane to fly from Great Britain to Australia. There were several conditions - the pilot and crew must be Australian, the machine British, and the flight of up to 15,000 miles, had to be completed in 720 hours and by 31st December 1920. This was undoubtedly difficult but with the new spirit of adventure that had entered aviation, British manufacturers and pilots, aided by the Air Ministry, were soon at work to see how it could be achieved.

The first away on the non-stop Atlantic attempt were Hawker and Mackenzie-Grieve who, grasping at a change in the weather, took off at 3.48pm on 18th May 1919. Just one hour later the Martinsyde team were ready to take off in

Alcock and Whitten Brown in their Vickers Vimy (a modified heavy bomber) slowly climb into the sky from St John's, Newfoundland in June 1919 to attempt the first non-stop trans-Atlantic crossing.

Thousands turn out to line the route and cheer as Alcock and Whitten Brown are greeted on their arrival in London and ceremoniously driven from Euston station to the Royal Aero Club in Piccadilly.

pursuit. Unfortunately their heavily fuel-laden aircraft slipped sideways and crashed as it started to climb. Raynham and Morgan suffered only minor injuries but the report of the crash added drama to newspaper accounts of the day's events. More drama was to follow because nothing else was heard of Hawker and Mackenzie-Grieve. After several days had elapsed, the press in Britain declared them dead and King George V made an announcement from Buckingham Palace expressing his sympathy at the tragic loss of 'One of the most able and daring pilots to sacrifice his life for the fame and honour of British flying.' The *Daily Mail* immediately announced that it would provide financial support for Hawker's wife and child. And the Air Ministry, in a masterly *volte-face*, issued a statement: 'To enjoin caution upon competitors rather than urge them to make the attempt.' The press, although restrained by today's standards, had a field day which was further enhanced by the news, on 25th May, that Hawker and Mackenzie-Grieve were alive and on board a steamship then off the Butt of Lewis. They had flown over halfway across the Atlantic before their engine started to

fail. With great presence of mind, Hawker searched for a ship, ditched his Sopwith aircraft in the path of a vessel and waited to be picked up. The ship had no wireless equipment nor passed close to another that had, therefore it had taken a week before information on the whereabouts of the airmen could be passed by visual signals to the shore. Fleet Street's purple prose aroused the public's tears of joy and a crowd of 100,000 thronged King's Cross station and its surrounds to greet the 'surviving heroes'. The King awarded both men the Air Force Cross and the *Daily Mail* divided £5,000 between them in recognition of their bravery and determination.

When Alcock and Brown took off for their attempt on 14th June it could have been an anti-climax except that now the public had been reminded of the possible fate that awaited them. The report of their successful landing in Ireland 16 hours and 12 mins after their departure was met with jubilation. They had flown non-stop 1,890 miles across water at an average speed of 118mph and proved the future direction of commercial aviation. Alcock and Brown's arrival in

London was met by similar crowds to that which had greeted Hawker and Mackenzie-Grieve. At a huge reception at the Savoy, Winston Churchill, in his capacity both as Secretary-of-State for War and Air and President of the Air Council, presented the *Daily Mail* prize plus subsidiaries totalling £13,000. In his speech Churchill referred to the fantastic strides forward which aviation had taken since Bleriot's uneasy crossing of the Channel only ten years before. Of the Atlantic achievement Churchill stated: 'Across this waste, through this obscurity, were two human beings, hurtling through the air, piercing the cloud and darkness, finding their unerring path in spite of every difficulty to their exact objective across those hundreds of miles where they arrived almost on scheduled time.' Churchill then informed Alcock and Brown that they were to be knighted by the King.

Coinciding with all this excitement was Britain's first Aerial Derby, flown at Hendon in the presence of a huge crowd. Public awareness of aviation and its perils was further heightened by reports of the abortive Schneider Trophy Contest for seaplanes held at Bournemouth which, due to various crashes in the prevailing fog, had finally had to be declared null and void. Then came the Air Ministry's announcement that it was to back Capt Ross Smith, of the Australian Flying Corps, to carry out a survey on the feasibility of a proposed route to Australia for the recently offered £A10,000 prize. Without any reliable information about landing facilities between

Calcutta and Port Darwin, it was decided that no competitor would be allowed to start until the Air Ministry was satisfied that conditions and facilities were to be, in some measure, practicable. Smith's optimistic report on the route prompted the Vickers company to propose that he be the pilot for their attempt; again with a Vimy bomber. Ross Smith immediately accepted and selected his brother Keith as co-pilot. There were, as with the trans-Atlantic flight, other competitors but it was the Smith brothers and their two crew who departed on 12th November 1919 and arrived safely on 10th December in Port Darwin, Australia. They had covered 11,135 miles over 29 days (136 flying hours) and, like their trans-Atlantic counterparts, were knighted by the King on their return; their two sergeant crew members also received suitable decorations. The success of this flight together with the accompanying tragedies that befell other competitors again presented the press with a feast of material and the public lapped it up. Long-distance overland flights such as this had the advantage of being reported daily via the newspapers' overseas correspondents and readers were encouraged to follow the airmen's progress. Press coverage was now no longer restricted to reportage but, with the appointment of proper aviation correspondents, freely extended to discussion and criticism of different types of aircraft, their engines and handling characteristics. In just one year after the Great War Trenchard saw what he had hoped for, a nation that was becomimg 'air-minded'.

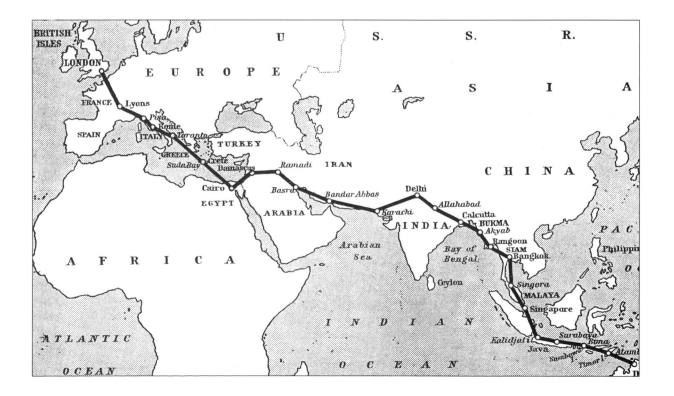

The main assembly area for the aircraft taking part in the 1920 RAF Aerial Pageant at Hendon.

Meanwhile, demobilised service pilots, anxious to remain in aviation and unable to find employment with aircraft manufacturers (hard hit by the loss of their wartime market), were joining forces to buy ex-RAF two-seater aeroplanes offered for sale at giveaway prices by the specially formed Aircraft Disposal Company. These aeroplanes, with slight degrees of modification and a new paint-job, were operated for 'joy rides' from farmers' fields all over the country. With a modest amount of advance publicity an aeroplane would visit a small town to introduce its citizens to the 'miracle of flight'. Further appearances were made at garden parties and fêtes with the occasional addition of some display flying. The importance of this activity was that it brought aviation to the populace and was at the root of a growing enthusiasm for the aeroplane. Civil aviation in a true commercial sense, as an alternative to travel by land or sea, got off to a ragged start in 1919 with most passenger aircraft offered largely comprising of converted military designs. Given the dramatic change in fortune of the aircraft manufacturers this was hardly surprising but the national railway strike of September 1919 allowed the embryonic air transport companies to show their true worth. For the first time, aircraft were carrying mails and newspapers between principal cities on a regular basis and ferrying company executives to and from their scattered industrial sites. Although the public had not yet become aware of the aeroplane as a faster alternative mode of transport, the strike episode proved it was relatively safe; a fact underlined by Avro's announcement that by late 1919 it had carried some 30,000 passengers without accident.

The onset of the 1920s saw the rise of the flying clubs and although some, like Cecil Pashley's at Shoreham, were founded as early as 1912, this was to become the decade of popular flying. Again, ex-RAF machines purchased for little money were adapted for the role and registered with civil letters as per the Air Navigation Act of 1919. Aerodromes, very often little more than large expanses of grass, were established throughout the country with hangars being erected alongside workshops for the attendant services. Most of the training expertise was provided by ex-service pilots; however, the Royal Aero Club records show that the majority of wartime flyers gave up aviation and a new generation of civil pilots was created by the clubs, many of whom would form the backbone of civil aviation as the 1920s progressed. The opening of the Imperial War Museum, at the Crystal Palace, in June 1920, with a large section devoted to Allied and enemy aircraft, gave the public a sense of reality to attach to the many war stories of 'derring-do' then being published. The real taste of military aviation came, however, with the RAF Aerial Pageant at Hendon in July (the first of the RAF's famous air displays). The purpose behind this air show was threefold: to show the public the latest developments and achievements of the RAF; to provide a focal point for excellence in flying; and to raise money for an RAF charity, the Memorial Fund. Some 40,000 people flocked to Hendon on Saturday, 3rd July 1920, and what they saw left them breathless with excitement: aerial dogfights, precision formation flying, supreme aerobatics and 'crazy' flying (with impossible skids, flat turns and imminent crashes), set-piece trench attacks and three large twin-engine transports hurtling towards the crowd to lift off only at the last moment. The show was an unqualified success and became a talking point for days. No sooner was Hendon over than the International Aero Exhibition opened at Olympia where every manufacturer displayed their latest designs of aeroplanes and engines together with a number of prototype ideas. This static exhibition was reported in *The Aeroplane*

were performance limitations, new ideas were constantly being sought to make aerobatic displays even more spectacular. Experiments with smoke trails were conducted by the RAF although it was quickly resolved that they had very little military relevance. However, when the smoke output was controlled it created lingering patterns in the sky marking the path of the aircraft and this was immediately adapted for aerobatic displays. Further experiments led, in May 1924, to the introduction of red smoke and Major J C Savage, using white smoke, invented the art of skywriting. Using a wartime SE5A for its high performance and manoeuvrability, he wrote single words often at a height of 10-12,000 feet and some two miles across.

Left - A time-exposed image of the patterns created by wing-tip lights in the night sky.

Right - The results of Major J C Savage's advertising 'skywriting' with white smoke trails.

as: 'A complete washout as a show intended to draw the great British public into aviation' but was counted as a great success both commercially and militarily with a great deal of interest and business from overseas visitors. July's feast of aviation events then continued at Hendon with the second postwar Aerial Derby, which again attracted some 11,000 people. Public demand was so great that this formula of summer events was to continue throughout the 1920s. Additions made to the RAF's annual display included a 'New Types Park', where selected prototype aircraft could be viewed prior to being flown in public for the first time.

Aerobatics or 'stunt' flying, as the press called it, was the key ingredient in any air show and the public delighted to see an aeroplane flown to the outer limits of its envelope. Given that there

Sponsored by companies to write brand names in the sky, he formed a company of ex-RFC pilots and fulfilled a tremendous demand for his services. For the 1925 Wembley Exhibition the RAF presented a night-fighter squadron in a nocturnal display using black painted aircraft with the perimeters of their wings and fuselages illuminated by tiny white lights. The squadron gave, as Charles W A Scott recalled in his aviation autobiography, *Scott's Book*, not only an aerobatic display but, by using pyrotechnics with lights switched off, simulated an attack on a fortified position inside the arena. All of this was, however, pure showbusiness and flown at extremely low level. Despite its success in thrilling the public, two seasons of these displays resulted in the destruction of five aircraft and the tragic death of one valuable pilot and were therefore discontinued.

Alan Cobham's specially modified (Jaguar powered) DH50 of the Imperial Airways Survey flight.

The year of 1924 witnessed the arrival of the pilot as a public personality. The first of the media 'heroes' was Alan Cobham who came to prominence as a successful race pilot and as chief pilot of the de Havilland Aeroplane Hire Service. Cobham, however, had ambitions to 'make the public air minded', and trading on his growing reputation persuaded Sir Sefton Brancker, the Director of Civil Aviation, that a forthcoming visit to India to examine the possibilities of establishing an airship link, would be more politically served if the trip was made by air rather than by P&O liner. Both Sefton Brancker and Lord Thomson, then Secretary-of-State for Air, supported the idea but only at the price of the steamship fare, which represented half the cost. Undaunted, Cobham proposed to de Havilland's that they should participate with their new DH50 passenger biplane and he would raise the rest via sponsored sources. This he managed and, in November 1924, departed from Stag Lane aerodrome with Brancker and an engineer for a 10-day, stage-by-stage, flight to Karachi and Rangoon. Cobham's return from the epic 18,000 mile flight at Croydon aerodrome in March 1925 was to the cheers of a welcoming crowd and the avid attention of Fleet Street's journalists and photographers. This was followed by a publicity flight for de Havilland taking off from Croydon at 5am to fly non-stop to Zurich, refuelling and returning to land at 5.30pm the same day.

That summer Cobham was busy piecing together his next great project, to fly to the Cape and back 'with ease'. Eventually organised under the banner of an Imperial Airways survey flight to investigate an air route to South Africa, he again flew the now re-engined DH50 and was sponsored by a whole host of companies including Sir Charles Wakefield's Castrol Oil. Cobham's departure in November 1925, complete with a cinematographer, was described by Fleet Street as: 'Pen in one hand and control stick in the other.' His arrival at Cape Town in February 1926, having covered 8,000 miles in 94 flying hours, was to a worldwide acclaim; Cobham having carefully dispatched reports from all his stopping points. An even greater wave of publicity greeted his return to England at the end of March and his triumphal landing at Croydon aerodrome was to the cheers of a seething crowd of thousands. Greeted by Sir Philip Sassoon, the Under Secretary-of-State for Air, Cobham was commanded to an audience with the King at Buckingham Palace. This was followed by Gordon Selfridge displaying the DH50 in his Oxford Street store, a live radio interview, the award of the Air Force Cross and the announcement that Cobham's next flight would be to Australia and back using the same aeroplane, only this time fitted with floats. Although this would be another 'first', the important aspect was to maximise publicity by returning to land the aircraft on the River Thames right outside the Houses of Parliament. Taking off from Rochester on the last day of June 1926, Cobham reached Port Darwin in 37 days where he changed the seaplane floats for a conventional undercarriage and flew on to Melbourne and Sydney. His flight was not without incident, including the death of his engineer, and full reports were dispatched to Fleet Street to feed an anxious public. Cobham's arrival in Australia was greeted as that of a 'god'. His return to London on the 1st of October was no less tumultuous. With a great sense of occasion he set himself to land on the Thames at 2.30pm on a Friday afternoon, timed to ensure both a large crowd and the weekend headlines. Received on the Speaker's Steps by the Secretary-of-State for Air and congratulated on his triumphant 24 day return flight, Alan Cobham was by that stage a household name. His immediate knighthood, his best-selling book *My Flight to the Cape and Back*, the cinema film of the survey trip and the press adulation achieved exactly what he wanted. Not only had the tremendous publicity put de Havilland firmly in the forefront to sell its new 'Cheap to buy and easy to fly' DH60 Moth biplane but the British public now warmly embraced aeroplanes and the intrepid exploits of the aviators.

During his Memorable Flight from England to Australia and back, Sir Alan Cobham wrote of

THE DUAL BURBERRY

" In Burma we were held up owing to the monsoon, and during our enforced halt it rained nearly five inches per day for five days. The natives seemed more interested in my Burberry Coat that stood up against the rain than in my wonderful little seaplane.

" The reversible idea was a huge success, because on landing I could quickly turn the coat inside-out and appear in a smart tweed fit for any occasion."

ALAN J. COBHAM.

There is a wide selection of patterns. Examples of materials and booklet illustrating the Dual Burberry sent post free. Please mention " Times Weekly."

BURBERRYS LTD. HAYMARKET, LONDON, S.W.1

The next of the media 'heroes', proclaimed during May 1927, was the previously unknown American, Charles Lindbergh. Sponsored by a group of St Louis businessmen, he flew his single-engine Ryan NYP monoplane alone for 33½ hours to cover the 3,590 miles from New York to Paris and claim the $25,000 Orteig Prize for the first non-stop flight between the two cities. Arriving at Le Bourget at 10.22pm on Saturday 21st, Lindbergh circled the 'confusing lights thrown up from the airport' before coming in to land in front of a vast cheering crowd. Although normally a reticent man, he was overwhelmed by the scale of public acclaim and was

tower where he mounted the ladder and showed himself to the crowd.' He was later taken to the US Embassy in London where the press had their opportunity to interrogate him about his flight. The universal acclaim that greeted Lindbergh led most people to believe that he was the first person to have flown across the Atlantic, thus eclipsing the achievement of Alcock and Brown. Among the growing band of aviation enthusiasts his flight was seen for what it really achieved: in a world still dominated by the biplane here was a small, single-engine monoplane, part-metal, part-fabric, which had been flown single-handed almost entirely on instru-

Charles Lindbergh and his Ryan NYP overwhelmed by crowds on his arrival at Croydon in May 1927.

forcefully propelled to 'front of stage' by the US Ambassador to France, who was anxious to manipulate the success for his country's prestige. The exercise was repeated on Sunday 29th when an enormous crowd waited to greet Lindbergh at Croydon. Such was the number of people clamouring to get a sight of him that he made two attempts to land before a pathway could be safely cleared. Then: 'A number of the regular aviation people fought their way to the machine and held the crowd off by sheer strength of arm and fist. Lindbergh wisely remained inside the machine or he might have been torn into souvenirs. Eventually a much battered car with Royal Aero Club officials and police arrived, extricated him, and ploughed to the control

ments. To the airminded public, Lindbergh's flight demonstrated not only the changing shape of the aeroplane but of aviation itself.

Following Lindbergh's major achievement came the September 1927 triumph of the RAF's Schneider Trophy seaplane race team in Venice, with its Supermarine S5 monoplane. Powered by a highly-tuned Napier Lion engine, the S5 was one of three different machines entered by Air Chief Marshal Sir Hugh Trenchard's 'High Speed Flight'. This victory, in the face of fierce competition, added considerably to Britain's prestige and vindicated Trenchard's belief that such competitions pushed forward the frontiers of design. The year 1928 saw an extensive list of aviation successes - among the more significant was that of Bert Hinkler who, in a modified prototype Avro Avian, landed at Darwin on 22nd February after a record-breaking 16 day solo flight from Croydon. Two days later Lady Heath, an imposing Irishwoman, was taking off from Johannesburg for the second leg of her solo flight from Cape Town to London. Flying a standard Avro Avian she arrived back at Croydon on 17th May and was quoted as saying that aviation was now so safe that: 'A woman can fly across Africa wearing a Parisian frock and keeping her nose powdered all the way.' Then, on 31st May, an Australian, Charles Kingsford Smith, with co-pilot Charles Ulm plus a navigator and wireless operator, took off from Oakland, California, in a Dutch-built Fokker tri-motor monoplane called the 'Southern Cross', for the first flight across the Pacific to Australia. Flying via Honolulu, Suva in Fiji and then on to Brisbane, Charles Kingsford Smith not only logged the longest sea crossing ever made by air (3,200 miles in 34 hours 30 mins) but with his Fokker transport also proved the viability of an air link between these two continents.

All these other aviation milestones were reported by the press but to a limited degree and it was not until the arrival of America's Amelia Earhart in June 1928 that Fleet Street found the next personality to project into the limelight. Her claim to fame as 'the first woman to fly the Atlantic' was largely an exercise in publicity masterminded by the New York publisher George Putnam. Amelia Earhart was merely a passenger in the Fokker tri-motor floatplane piloted by Wilmer Stultz with Lou Gordon as his engineer; but it was all that was needed to make the claim. She was selected for the flight from a number of possible candidates and although a qualified pilot, had been tutored for the role by Putnam who took great care in establishing what he considered the right image. Presenting Earhart as the epitome of style, beauty and daring, Putnam suggested to the press that the Americans were likening her to Lindbergh and reports coining the nickname 'Lady Lindy' soon appeared. The existence of the pilot and the navigator who flew the aeroplane (from Newfoundland to Burry Port, Carmarthen and then on to Southampton) was, needless to say, carefully brushed aside. The public, aided by the press and Putnam's publicity machine, immediately took 'Lady Lindy' to their hearts. She dominated the news, to the detriment of other aviators, until her return to America to promote the George Putnam book about her flight, *20 Hours 40 Minutes*, and to attend a huge round of prearranged civic receptions and a lecture tour.

A publicity photograph commissioned by George Putnam to project Amelia Earhart in the 'Lady Lindy' mould.

Under the rules of the Schneider Trophy contest the victors were to host the next event, thus, 1929 brought the full glare of Schneider publicity to Britain. Venice, although a substantial success for British aeroplanes and the RAF, was remote from the general public. With the contest set for the Solent in the autumn, there was a whole six months or more for the press to build the public interest. Played on an international stage, patriotism for the British team was fierce and, although all the team members were serving RAF officers and should have remained anonymous, the press did its best to translate them into identifiable personalities. The airframe and engine manufacturers, with much to gain from the publicity, entered freely into the euphoria that began to build. By the summer an early form of merchandising emerged with packets of tea, bookmarks and other ephemera endorsing the British entry with images of the pilots and their racing seaplanes. Came 'race' day on 7th September 1929 and everybody who was anybody in aviation plus Edward, the Prince of Wales, gathered in the Solent. The sea was 'awash with yachts and small craft' bearing spectators while the coastline around the course and over on the Isle of Wight was thronged with thousands of spectators. To win on home ground had become a point of pride for the British and the press elevated the status of a win to an almost warlike significance for victory.

Fortunately the public was not let down and Fg Off H R Waghorn in the Rolls-Royce powered Supermarine S6 easily won. Three days later, using the same seaplane, Sqn Ldr A H Orlebar raised the world speed record to an astounding 355.8mph. The British public now not only had its 'heroes of the air' but believed that British aeroplanes and engines dominated the world; to the extent of the winning aircraft's fast aerodynamic lines appearing in designs for fabrics, car radiator mascots and various souvenirs.

At the end of the decade aviation had become a major growth industry and for pilots it was no longer easy to attain individual achievements - the vast costs involved demanding sponsorships that had become difficult to secure. It was against this changing background that Fleet Street discovered its next heroine in the shape of Amy Johnson, an unlikely young woman from Hull who worked as a secretary and used her own salary to learn to fly. Amy was likeable, modest and very hardworking: 'She used to rise at 5.0am for an hour's flying before being at her office at 9.0am - in the evenings she was either back at the aerodrome or studying engines.' Amy had a dream to set up a personal solo record from London to Australia and, aware that this would require some degree of self-sufficiency, she studied to become Britain's first licensed female ground engineer. Aided by her father and

The victorious 1929 RAF High Speed Flight team's record breaking Supermarine S6 at Calshot.

"Amy, Wonderful Amy"

SOLO LONDON - TO - AUSTRALIA
BRITAIN'S BRAVEST YOUNG LADY PILOT

THE WHOLE WORLD
IS SINGING HER PRAISES

London: **FRANCIS, DAY & HUNTER, Ltd.**
138-140 Charing Cross Road, London W.C.2.

Authorised for Sale only in the British Empire
excepting Canada, Australia & New Zealand

1/- NET

AT YOUR LOCAL MUSIC STORE

finally sponsored by Lord Wakefield, Amy purchased a secondhand Gipsy Moth, overhauled the engine, painted it green and named it 'Jason'. With only 90 hours solo time and having never flown further than 200 miles, she took off from Croydon on 5th May 1930 - with a spare propeller lashed to the aeroplane - for her 12,000 mile adventure. At first ignored by the press, her safe arrival in Vienna made Fleet Street realise that here was a story in the making: 'Glamorous unknown typist dares to challenge Bert Hinkler's record.' In reality Amy Johnson did not set out to challenge anyone but by the time she had reached Calcutta she was two days ahead of Hinkler and had set a new record. Congratulated by the Secretary-of-State for Air, Lord Thomson, Amy became headline news and, manipulating a series of unfortunate landings into a 'will she, won't she?' drama, the *Daily Mail* bought the rights to her story for £2,000. Approaching the final sea crossing to Australia she slipped two days behind Hinkler and then was reported 'lost'. The public's heart missed a beat but within 24 hours she was 'found', having landed on an island where there were no modern communications. On 24th May she landed at Port Darwin to tumultuous cheers from the local crowd and to international acclaim as a 'heroine of the air'. Two days later in Sydney, Amy was greeted by an overwhelming crowd, awarded a CBE from the King and was the recipient of C G Grey's comment that

her arrival in Australia was 'By pluck and luck rather than good aeronautical judgement.' Any manufacturer who had anything to do with the Gipsy Moth or Miss Johnson jumped on the bandwagon of publicity. The *Daily Mail* extended its rights offer to £10,000 to include the purchase of the aeroplane, a national tour on her return and her services as a journalist on aviation topics. Amy Johnson, in a mere 19 days, secured for herself a place in history and a future in aviation. When she returned to Britain they were singing 'Amy Wonderful Amy' in all the music halls and the sheet music had already become a best-seller.

The British public were by now becoming somewhat blasé about aviation achievements and the Government, beset by a deep recession, refused to participate in the forthcoming 1931 Schneider Trophy Contest. Rescued by the patriotic generosity of Lady Houston, this prestigious event then turned into a 'one horse race' with none of the other competing countries able to field an entry by the required date. The RAF's 'High Speed Flight' flew the course on 13th September in an S6B, a modification of their previous winner, to secure the Trophy for all time. Then, on 29th September, Flt Lieut G H Stainforth in the same S6B raised the world speed record to 407.5mph, a considerable feat; but in the rapidly developing world of aviation it seemed like just another statistic.

The Air League of the British Empire had been in existence since April 1909 with the express aim of: 'Educating the citizens of the British Empire as well as the authorities entrusted with the defence of it, to the vital importance of air power both from a commercial as well as from a national defence point of view.' Funded by the subscriptions of its members, the League was largely a political lobby that served the country well during the First World War and during the

Air Commodore A Chamier of the Air League.

formation of the RAF in 1917-18. It was also significant in focusing the Government's attention to the shortfall of home air defences during the early 1920s; however, by the end of the decade it seemed to have lost its way and become the butt of much criticism. With the appointment of Air Cdre J A Chamier as Chairman in 1932 all that changed and the 'Air League', as it became known, was applied to a more practical development of the movement for airmindedness first inspired by Alan Cobham in 1925. Not that it lost its political origins; Chamier was most forceful in pressing for the expansion and re-equipping of the RAF with the most advanced aircraft possible, but he realised that the future of air power lay with the force of popular opinion.

Alan Cobham had already turned his attention directly to the public, which he believed was not airminded at all, and created the 'National Aviation Day Campaign'. This was a flying circus display which flew Cobham's collection of aeroplanes to the limits of their envelopes, staged special items such as free-fall parachuting and crazy flying and took as many people as possible for '5 shilling joy rides'. In reality there was no 'National' day because the circus was on tour and during 1932 Cobham visited 168 venues with his show. During his first year, over half-a-million spectators attended, and of these some 60,000 flew as 'joy riding' passengers. Chamier was quick to realise the value of Cobham's campaign and the Air League, although not financially involved, officially supported the tour. What Chamier wanted, however, was something truly national and, now elevated to Secretary-General of the League, he began to put his plans for an Empire Air Day into operation. The concept was simple: that all aerodromes, both military and civil, should open their doors on the same single day each year, allowing the public freedom to explore the workings of an aerodrome and to examine the aircraft, while allowing the professional pilots a chance to display their flying prowess. It took a great deal of tact and persuasion to gain acceptance for this scheme and the first Empire Air Day did not take place until 26th May 1934, when 39 military air stations and most of the principal civil aerodromes took part. Alan Cobham was by this time into the third season of his campaign and his success attracted several imitators.

Chamier also addressed himself to the youth of Britain and put forward proposals to form a junior section of the Air League. It came to his attention that there was a growing band of scale-

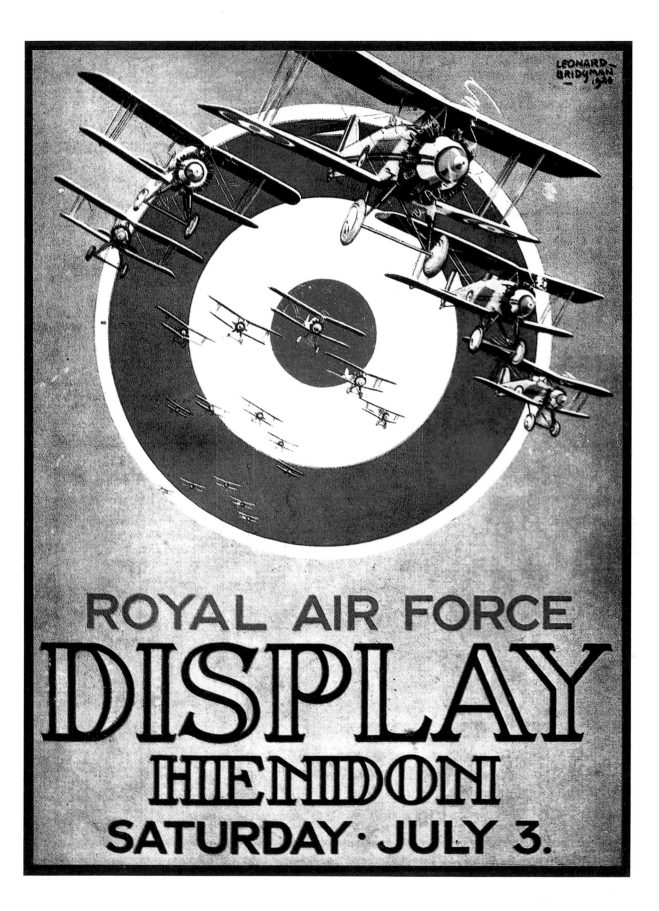

A Leonard Bridgman poster, depicting Armstrong Whitworth Siskin Mk IIIs, commissioned for the 1926 annual display of the RAF at Hendon (initially the RAF Tournament and then the RAF Aerial Pageant).

PLATE 3.

THE HAWKER HENLEY

THE TIPSY TWO SEATER

Two examples of the Howard Leigh postcards given to junior members of the Air League of the British Empire.
(from the 1938 Air Leaguers' Album of British Aircraft)

PLATE 4.

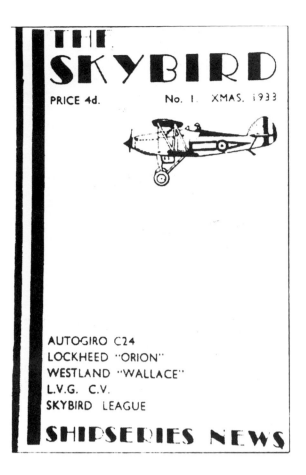

THE SKYBIRD

PRICE 4d.   No. 1. XMAS. 1933

AUTOGIRO C24
LOCKHEED "ORION"
WESTLAND "WALLACE"
L.V.G. C.V.
SKYBIRD LEAGUE

SHIPSERIES NEWS

A typical highly finished Skybird 1/72 scale solid wood model of a 1917 Nieuport scout.

model aircraft enthusiasts. Some were organised into small groups but had no national leadership and many of them were scratch building due to the paucity of plans, kits or technical information. Mindful that 'The boy is the father of the man', Chamier realised it was vital their interest be nurtured and developed, yet it was outside the Air League's brief to do so. Fortunately their cause was championed by Sir Harry Brittain, the entrepreneur and philanthropist, who was conducting his own 'airmindedness' campaign directed at industry. With Sir Harry as its President, the 'Skybird League' was formed in 1933 on the back of a commercial decision to market solid scale-model kits of all current aeroplanes, plus some of the more famous types from the past, and to update the range as new prototypes were revealed or came into production. The kits were supplied in 1/72 scale, partially shaped out of hardwood and complete with detailed plans and technical information about the actual aeroplane. They were designed to be finished to a high degree of detail and as accurate as possible to the real thing. Skybird modellers were recruited into a local Skybird League modelling group - sometimes affiliated to an RAF squadron - which would compete nationally with the standard of its modelling for prizes and trophies. The Skybird League also published *The Skybird*, a regular newsletter which featured

the models in and out of production and supplied further details, drawings and descriptions of current aeroplanes so that modellers could incorporate the latest variants into their work. Skybird League clubs formed throughout Britain reached a total of over 350 with yet more overseas. Chamier ensured that the Air League became involved in both the Skybird Clubs and the flying model associations by donating Air League prizes and making a great many personal appearances to present trophies and to talk about the future of air power.

Within two years aeromodelling, both solid and flying, became a large business with several manufacturers (including the brand FROG - 'Flies Right Off the Ground') competing for a share of the market. Some powered models had miniature petrol engines and there were learned discussions on the technicalities of radio control. To cater for the market, a new magazine, *The Aero Modeller*, was launched in 1933 and incorporated *The Skybird*. Chamier also chose this moment to launch his junior 'Air Leaguers' scheme using *The Aero Modeller* as its official journal; the League's own publication *Air Review* remained reserved for senior members. In addition to a series of Air Leaguer activities and free entrance to Empire Air Day displays, members received a monthly issue of postcard-size reproductions of Howard Leigh gouaches depicting British aeroplanes. These were collected into specially supplied albums and then highly prized. Members were also required to sign a promise that included: 'To help my country in every way to take a leading place in the air and to give service when opportunity occurs.' And: 'To interest myself in aviation and to learn all I can about it.' Air Cdre Chamier judged the mood of Britain's youth correctly and his scheme moved from strength to strength, being the foundation stone of the Air Defence Cadet Corps which ultimately became the Air Training Corps (ATC).

AIR DEFENCE OF GREAT BRITAIN
COMMAND EXERCISES

The RAF had, since its formation, conducted annual Air Exercises in the same way as the other two Services and by 1930 these developed into national proportions with clearly stated defenders and aggressors, the latter representing a 'Continental' power. A large area of Britain was divided into two fictional countries, designated 'Northland' and 'Southland', with fighter and bomber squadrons divided to act as opposing Red and Blue forces. Battle was enacted under a specific set of rules over a period of up to four days, including nights, and the whole process scored by strategically positioned 'umpires' both in the air and on the ground. The object was twofold: to test and experiment with defence tactics and strategy, and to assess the performances of the machines and the men.

Daily press communiqués via the Air Ministry allowed the progress of these 'battles' to be followed. But, after political criticism of the RAF based on press reports, 1931 saw a security clamp down on journalists in the field, although some managed to fly with the bombing groups. In 1932, following the previous year's poor fighter interceptions of invading bomber forces, it was decided that there were distinct advantages to advanced intelligence. And the Observer Corps, the direct descendant of Ashmore's Metropolitan Observer Service, which had been slowly evolving throughout the 1920s, was now given a prominent role to play. Fighters were kept at 'scramble' readiness until the enemy was spotted, at which time they were supplied with Observer Corps reported co-ordinates, height

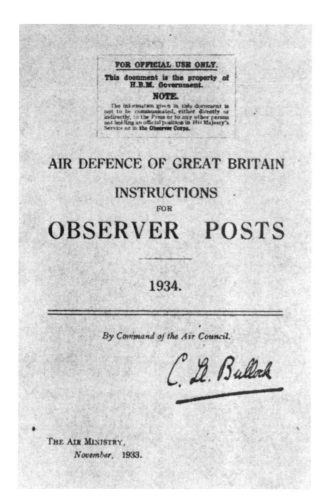

AIR DEFENCE OF GREAT BRITAIN

INSTRUCTIONS

FOR

OBSERVER POSTS

1934.

By Command of the Air Council.

C. L. Bullock

THE AIR MINISTRY,
November, 1933.

and a projected course via their Command Centre. The problem came with the accuracy of the information supplied since reports were only visual or by sound locator with an 'observer's' own interpretation of height. Although Observer Corps activities had been controlled by the Air Ministry since 1929 and its area of coverage considerably expanded, it was still manned by part-time volunteers designated 'special constables' and training exercises - often without aircraft - were only undertaken six times a year. Prior to the 1933 Air Exercises, the RAF decided to introduce a new map grid system to simplify co-ordinates and an experimental intercommunication link was tried between an Observer Corps Centre and adjacent posts to verify height reports. A 'height checker' was also designated, his role being to correct heights by applying basic geometry to the various reports. All of this proved very unsatisfactory since an incorrect height could result in the reported map position being wildly inaccurate and intercepting fighters failing to locate the aggressor. Work had been in progress to develop an instrument, first called a 'height bar', which would allow accuracy at any angle of observation by any individual. This showed promise and during the 1933 Exercises a much revised version, a MK IIA instrument, was tested at selected Observer Corps posts and proved to be quite accurate.

Lessons learnt from previous Air Defence Command Exercises, combined with a rapidly changing political climate on the Continent, led the Air Ministry to press the Government for an expansion of the RAF and to issue contract specifications for more advanced fighter designs. In July 1934, following considerable pressure, especially from Winston Churchill, the Government issued a directive that conceded these demands. The expansion was to include 31 additional Home Defence squadrons and a realignment of Britain's air defence strategy. For the Observer Corps this meant a dramatic increase in size, with a reorientation to extend considerably further north and to expand its coverage in the east, also filling in the gaps in the south. The Air Exercises of that same month followed much the pattern of previous years including a now unrealistic scenario; plans having been made well ahead of the Government's

The 'Special Constables' of Welwyn Garden City Observer Corps post, 17 Group, on exercise in 1933.

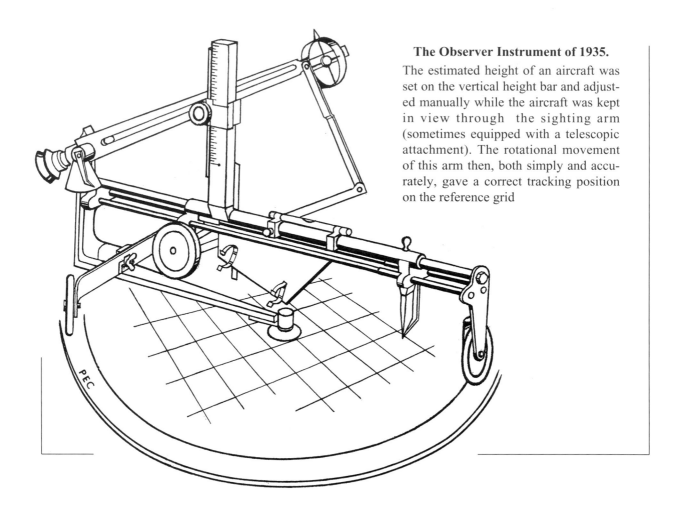

The Observer Instrument of 1935.
The estimated height of an aircraft was set on the vertical height bar and adjusted manually while the aircraft was kept in view through the sighting arm (sometimes equipped with a telescopic attachment). The rotational movement of this arm then, both simply and accurately, gave a correct tracking position on the reference grid

announcement. They were, however, of particular value to the Observer Corps who had a chance to experiment more fully with their 'Height Calculator', checking the information obtained from the MK IIA against a further developed MK IIB, with its relative ease of use.

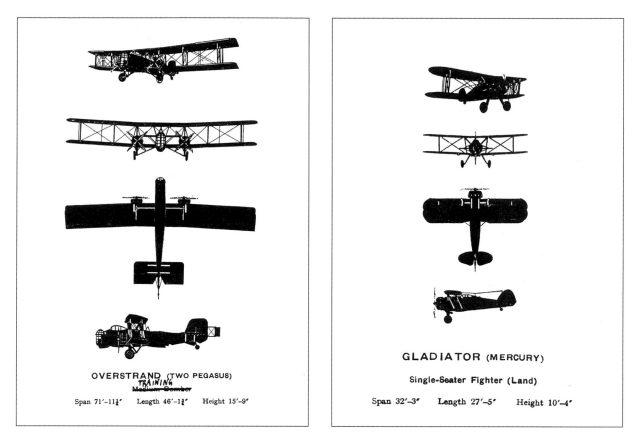

OVERSTRAND (TWO PEGASUS)
TRAINING
Medium Bomber

Span 71'–11¼'   Length 46'–1¾'   Height 15'–9'

GLADIATOR (MERCURY)

Single-Seater Fighter (Land)

Span 32'–3"   Length 27'–5"   Height 10'–4"

Typical silhouette pages from the early A.P.1480.

Reports during the Air Exercise praised the Observer Corps for its speed of observation reporting and its accuracy. But the results were retained by the Air Ministry and not divulged.

March 1935 saw the formation of the first six new Observer Corps Groups out of the 16 that were planned and the thousands of new observers that were needed. This move went hand-in-hand with the development of plotted 'Radio-location', which had now proved to be a practical consideration and was proposed as a supplement to the Observer Corps as an early warning system for longer range detection. The Army, whose experiments with massive coastal sound locators in 1934 completely failed, presented a 'fixed azimuth' system to work out the enemy's position from multiple reports of height and bearing. This, although well thought out, was complex and required a primitive computer (the 'Fruit Machine') to process the co-ordinates. This was both expensive to develop and time consuming in operation, although a modified version would later become an integral part of the radio-location network. The Air Defence Committee, therefore, turned the idea down and the Observer Corps' relatively simple MK IIB Height Calculator was adopted as standard issue, with the Army using small sound locators

attached to its searchlight and anti-aircraft batteries to aid sighting, particularly at night.

Aircraft location and position were all very well but in this sudden spurt of 'airmindedness' by the Services little thought was given to aircraft recognition. In late 1933 the Air Ministry produced a loose-leaf book of silhouettes, A.P.1480, but the silhouettes were both limited and crude, and, since no request for information had been asked of the overseas intelligence agencies, the loose-leaf book contained few of the aircraft that might be considered a threat. The distribution of A.P.1480 was initially restricted but common sense prevailed and, by 1935, all Observer Corps posts and regular Army anti-aircraft batteries were issued with at least one copy. There was, however, no official recognition training and neither was any required since the prime duty of the Observer Corps remained, as in 1918, to report 'all aircraft movements'. Specific analysis was still to be left to the RAF's Command Centres apart from the 'request' to differentiate between fighters and bombers. A further anomaly was the sudden realisation that observers were not subject to eyesight tests. A sample group proved to be below a 'required' standard and a new argument ensued between senior Observer Corps officers and the Air Ministry about rejection for

DE HAVILLAND "LEOPARD-MOTH" (Great Britain). The need of an aeroplane for sporting or touring use and embodying the comforts of a saloon car naturally followed the growth of private flying. The popular "Leopard-Moth," designed for this purpose, is a light cabin monoplane with a cruising speed of 119 m.p.h., and seating accommodation for three people, the pilot in front and two passengers side by side behind. The first appearance of this machine coincided with its entry in the King's Cup Race in 1933, which it won, piloted by its designer, Capt. Geoffrey de Havilland. (No. 13.)

DE HAVILLAND "LEOPARD MOTH"

HANDLEY PAGE "HERACLES" CLASS (Great Britain). This air liner is probably the most luxurious of its type. Used by Imperial Airways on both the European and Empire routes, it has accommodation for thirty-eight passengers and a crew of four, consisting of a Captain, Chief Officer and two Stewards. The interior is divided into two compartments with lavatories and buffet facilities in the centre. On the London–Paris route, luncheon and other meals are provided. Cruising speed is 95—105 m.p.h., and with four engines there is little possibility of forced landings through engine trouble. (No. 14.)

HANDLEY PAGE

BRITISH KLEMM "EAGLE" (Great Britain). A beautiful machine in appearance, the "Eagle" is also one with an exceptionally good performance, its speed being 148–170 m.p.h. according to the engine fitted. It is a low-wing cabin monoplane and has the advantage of a retractable undercarriage. A feature of the machine is the comfortable cabin which, it is claimed, is free from noise and draught and affords a good view to the two passengers and pilot. The doors on each side give easy entrance and exit. Although the "Eagle" is designed for touring it is sufficiently strong to perform aerobatics with grace and ease. (No. 15.)

BRITISH KLEMM "EAGLE"

a low standard of 'visual acuity' versus the already difficult problems of recruitment for the volunteer Corps.

While the Air Ministry restricted the copies of AP.1480 available, the public sector via the tobacco manufacturers were doing better with the distribution of cards on aviation subjects. Cigarette cards had been avidly collected by youngsters since they proliferated in the early 1920s and by the 1930s were available on a variety of specialist subjects appealing to both adult and youth. Thus, as Britain became more airminded it was inevitable that cigarette cards would follow suit. Although there were two early aviation sets produced, one in 1910 and the other in 1915, it was 1926-27 that saw the first of the many different sets that were to proliferate. The 1929 'Types of Aeroplanes' was the first specifically to portray and describe current aircraft but by 1935 there had been eight different sets on the subject, some with 54 cards in the set, covering military, civil and sporting aircraft both from Britain and abroad. Often beautifully produced with highly-detailed colour artwork - and one set with rudimentary silhouettes included on the reverse together with the technical and performance data - they were designed to be fixed into specially printed albums which repeated and enhanced the text on their reverse. Cigarette cards, together with the various books that were being published (e.g. the *Wonder* series) very often meant that members of the public were better informed on aircraft recognition than members of the Observer Corps or the Army's anti-aircraft units. This in turn produced a new type of aviation enthusiast, the 'aero spotter', who, like his railway equivalent, would diligently make up a notebook and, gleaning technical information wherever possible, would attempt to see and log all variants of an aircraft type, both military and civil. These activities were complementary to scale aeromodelling and to Air League activities and if a boy was involved in one aspect of aviation, he would very often become involved with another.

During the early 1930s public interest and confidence in aeroplanes, both as public transport and as a vital part of Britain's armed forces, was no longer in doubt. Aircraft development, urged on by advanced military planning, was moving apace and aviators themselves were still striving to break yet more records and extend the fron-

tiers of the aeroplane. A noteworthy example was the 1933 Houston Everest Expedition, sponsored by the redoubtable Lady Houston, in which an RAF Flight of two Houston-Westland PV.3 biplanes, with cameramen in the rear cockpits and headed by Air Cdre P Fellowes, flew at over 31,000 feet to film and photograph the summit of Mount Everest. Then in 1934 came the International Victorian Centenary Air Race from England to Australia for a £A10,000 prize sponsored by Sir Macpherson Robertson. The most significant aspect of this race was the de Havilland DH88 Comet which won in a startling race time of 70 hours 54 mins 12 secs between Mildenhall and Melbourne. The Comet, as were the Schneider Trophy winners, was designed and built specially for this race, in which three examples were entered following their development from scratch in just nine months. Powered by two special high-compression DH Gipsy Six 'R' engines producing 230hp, the Comet reached a top speed of 220mph and a range of 2,925 miles with a crew of two. Its sleek racing profile with thin tapered wings heralded a major advance in aeroplane design and set the shape of aircraft of the future. Compared with the front-line machines of the RAF, the Comet seemed light years ahead and proved what the aircraft manufacturers could achieve if design was not fettered by over complex and precise Air Ministry specifications. The press now had a new hero, the Comet itself, and although Charles W A Scott and Tom Campbell Black were well fêted for their win it was de Havilland's creation that

Tired but jubilant, Scott and Campbell Black arrive at Melbourne in their winning DH 88 Comet.

The changing shape of aeroplanes - Captain Edgar Percival, the designer (in a trilby hat which he always wore), piloting his highly successful aerodynamic Mew Gull racer over Bedfordshire.

claimed the glory. This well suited the directors of Grosvenor House in London's Park Lane who had sponsored the Scott and Black entry and after whose hotel one of the aeroplanes was named. Like the Supermarine S6B Schneider winner, the elegant fast shape of the Comet captured the imagination of the public and it too, with a sense of patriotic pride, found its way into designs and ephemera of the period. The difference was that, whereas the racing seaplane had been viewed as a sports aircraft, the Comet was a landplane with a carrying capacity and the press readily projected Comet-style airliners that would soon fill the skies. Inspired by the success of the Comet other aircraft manufacturers began

to view aerodynamic design (as opposed to building an aeroplane around its powerplant) in a new light. And, although compromise and trade off were essential ingredients between the drawing board and production requirements, new sleek shapes began to appear.

By the end of 1935 the 'airmindedness' campaigners, aware that the original aims were largely met, began to change the emphasis into the more practical aspects of aviation. Alan Cobham had completed his third year of air circus tours and claimed to have flown over 990,000 'joyriders' but announced that this was the last season and time for change. Attempts were still being made by individuals to set new records but they attracted little attention. A cartoon in *Popular Flying* for 1935, depicts a jubilant pilot who, on landing in Africa, is being treated with disdain by a native. Sneering from behind the bone in his nose, the native is telling the pilot 'Yes - I know, you did it on Shell.' At the Air League, Air Cdre Chamier continued to build on his success and formed a 'Pou Club' to promote affordable flying with a homebuild aeroplane, the 'Pou de Ciel', popularised as 'The Flying Flea'. This aeroplane comprised a plywood fuselage which carried a large rudder, engine, wheels and the lower and smaller of two upswept tandem wings. The upper mainplane was pivoted on its front spar and tilted for longitudinal control and there were no ailerons, turns being made on the rudder which was operated by sideways movement of the control column. Its French Designer, Henri Mignet, claimed that anyone who could build a packing case could build a 'Pou' and teach himself to fly it. This was the very spirit of airmindedness and in collaboration with Mignet, Chamier produced a special Air League home constructor's book complete with plans and built one himself - its 'unlikely' silhouette a bizarre (and soon to be proved, fatal) addition to the English skies.

**'If the British Empire is to become
an Air Power of international importance,
control by Airmen must immediately take
the place of that now occupied by Chairmen.'**

Air Cdre P Fellowes - 1934

READINESS FOR WAR

From the moment that Hitler elevated himself into absolute power in 1933 the Air Ministry became wary of an imminent programme of German re-armament. The substance of Hitler's speeches and the declared aims of his National Socialist Party were overtly to take back that territory which had been lost as a result of defeat in the First World War but, reading between the lines, his ambitions seemed far greater. Winston Churchill, from a backbench seat in the House of Commons, warned that Germany was, 'In violation of the Treaty of Versailles, busy creating an air force under the guise of flying clubs, police units and commercial ventures that would soon equal and outrival the RAF.' The MacDonald-Baldwin Government of National Coalition, with disarmament and pacifism at the centre of its policy, failed to see either a German military programme developing or to sense Hitler's determination to return Germany to the status of a major European power. Stanley Baldwin, for the Government, repudiated Churchill stating: 'Germany, can produce rapidly, if she chooses, aircraft and men but a country which for many years has possessed no military air force starts under a heavy handicap and it must be some time before it can equal in efficiency the RAF.' It was against such blinkered thinking that in March 1935 Reich Chancellor Adolf Hitler and Generalleutnant Hermann Goering felt sufficiently secure to announce the formation of the Reichsluftwaffe with a strike power equal to the RAF. Goering was made commander in chief of the Reichsluftwaffe and Erhard Milch, former head of Deutsche Lufthansa, became responsible for its development. Under their command were some 20,000 officers and men, and 1,888 aircraft - which were being added to at the rate of 200, and then 300, per month. Compared to the RAF's front-line strength of 1,170 aircraft, Hitler's announcement confirmed Churchill's worst fears and despite the fact that many politicians refused to believe that Germany was a possible enemy he stated, 'We are not faced with the prospect of a new war, but with something very like the resumption of the war that ended in 1918.' An official visit to Berlin by Anthony Eden and Sir John Simon (immediately following Hitler's announcement) confirmed the situation and with the 'threat' now more real than mythical, the Government did an about turn and asked the Air Ministry for a radical revision of its plans for the expansion of the RAF.

The emergence of the Luftwaffe could be traced back to the 1920s revival of the German air society, 'Deutscher Luftfahrtverband' (DLV), with gliding as its main activity to circumvent the Treaty of Versailles ruling on formalised flying. It was inside the DLV that all flying skills and training were fostered as the Paris Air Agreement of 1926 severely restricted the numbers of German military personnel who were allowed to fly. Co-operation with the German Transport Ministry provided another means of training these military pilots and secret sections of the Lufthansa commercial flying schools were also producing civil crews capable of military deployment. From the late 1920s on, Germany was probably the most airminded nation in Europe and its civil aircraft manufacturers were at last allowed to return to production - in fact they had never ceased, merely relocating to Sweden, Denmark, Turkey, Italy and Switzerland. In 1928 Goering, then a Reichstag deputy, pledged his support for Lufthansa and by the end of that year the DLV, now overtly paramilitary and flying some powered aircraft, registered 50,000 active members plus a large youth movement. By the early 1930s German aircraft design began to take on military specifications and in 1933 fast trainers were replaced by military fighters openly sporting machine-

Two of the posters produced to recruit the youth of Hitler's Germany into the Nazified paramilitary flying association 'Deutscher Luftfahrtverband' (DLV) - renamed as the 'Luftsport-Verband' in 1933.

guns. These fighters were ostensibly for defensive use, albeit in contravention of the now unenforcable Treaty of Versailles, while under the guise of commercial aviation, other developments were taking place. In 1934 the Heinkel He 70, a high-speed, single-engine, six-seat monoplane, made its début. It was first presented as a record breaker and then as a mail carrier but, with cramped accommodation and a high payload capacity, it was in truth a fast light bomber. The He 70 was of all-metal construction, had a retractable undercarriage and sleek aerodynamic lines and was far in advance of anything being flown by the RAF. Even more significant was the revelation that this aeroplane had been designed for production line manufacture, at a time when the British aircraft industry was still constructing individual aeroplanes by hand. The He 70 was followed in 1935 by the long-range, twin-engine Heinkel He 111 transport, designated for commercial use by Lufthansa. Then by the twin-engine Junkers Ju 86 which, like the He 111, had been secretly designed to military specifications but was initially passed off as a civil airliner.

In London the Air Ministry was well aware of these developments; it was with the benefit of detailed information supplied by Military Intelligence that they pressed hard for an expansion of the RAF. Most urgent of all was the need for a dramatic increase in the budget for the Air Estimates to allow British manufacturers to proceed, at all speed, with designs for new high-performance defensive fighters. The lessons learned during the First World War and from the various tactics tried in the annual Air Exercises, had firmly convinced the Air Ministry that 'The bomber will always get through.' Unaware that

'See, as the dawn arrives, our man has built the Luftwaffe' - a 1936 caricature of Goering by his principal staff officer, Ernst Udet.

German strategy would be to utilise its air force for short-range bombing strikes as a prelude to attack and occupation by ground forces, the Air Ministry placed its emphasis on home defence. This thinking was reinforced by the natural barriers of the English Channel and the North Sea, both of which demanded a range for hostile aircraft that would preclude surprise attacks. Germany's concentration on twin-engine bombers was also viewed as a possible development programme for enlarged four-engine versions, with much greater payloads and range. In the clandestine atmosphere that surrounded the German aircraft manufacturers, it would have been reasonably easy to reach the production

The 1934 record-breaking, high-speed, all-metal, Heinkel He 70 'Blitz' in its black and silver livery.

stage while the League of Nations looked on blindly.

The British plan, therefore, was that the strategic lessons learned in several years of the Air Exercises should now be put into practice. This required an expanded Observer Corps that could identify (as distinct from recognise) and fix the position of enemy raiders and pass that information, with great speed, to the RAF, who would 'scramble' its new generation of high-performance fighters to intercept. Additionally, the RAF would relay this information to the Army so that their anti-aircraft barrages would be ready to shoot down or divert enemy aircraft as directed by a centralised command. Much of this strategy was the same as that of the First World War, except both personnel and equipment had changed considerably and a degree of experience and testing had proved it worked. In contrast, the Germans, unable so far to stage any significant air exercises in collaboration with their ground forces, had no such experience from which to define a strategy and their escalating political ideology left little requirement for a policy of home defence.

On behalf of the British people, the irrepressible Lady Houston, worried by the Government's apparent refusal to respond to the 'worsening situation', renewed her offer to the Secretary-of-State for Air to advance £200,000 towards the costs of establishing a proper air defence of London, which she considered to be undefended. This time her generosity was refused, being seen as a direct attack on the MacDonald/Baldwin administration and their brand of pacifism. In any event her offer would have proved of little practical use, since the factual disclosures of Germany's rapidly growing military strength had already considerably changed the Government's attitude to defence. The problem now was not the cost but the time needed to implement the plans that, unbeknown to Lady Houston, had already been made. For the interim both the RAF and the Army, hampered by a lack of personnel and machines, were restricted to theoretical experiments in the Air Defence of Great Britain (ADGB).

By late 1935 it was evident that neither the rate of the planned expansion of the Observer Corps nor its extent was going to be adequate to meet

The British Army on exercise with sound locators in the mid-1930s - (despite a questionable accuracy sound locators operated with searchlights as the only method of directing anti-aircraft fire at night).

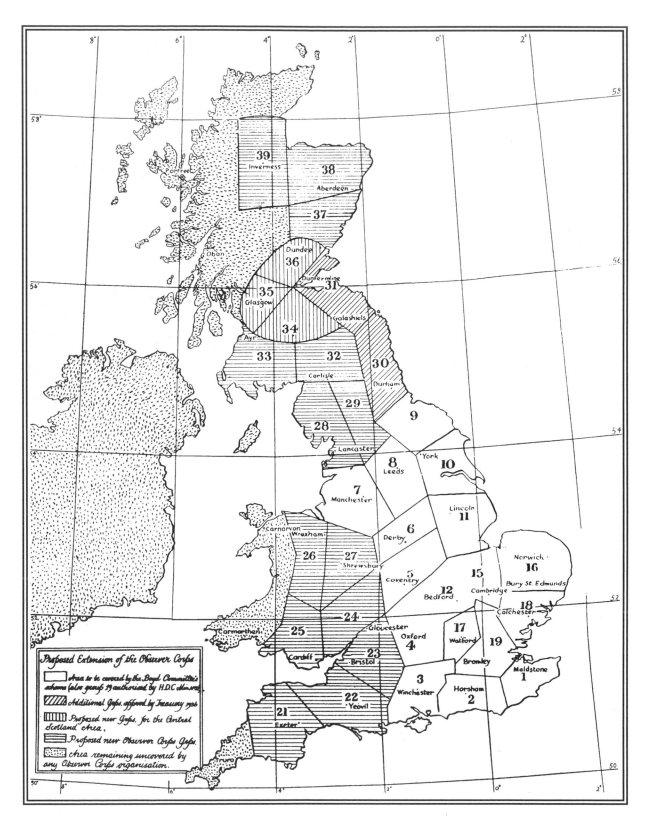

Official Air Ministry map detailing the proposed expansion of the Observer Corps.

the demands of the annual air exercises, let alone to aid the defence of Britain in time of war. A series of meetings and reports took place between the Home Office (under whose jurisdiction volunteer observers still remained as police specials) and the Air Ministry. This resulted in an agreement to accelerate the completion of a revised expansion programme, by two years, to March 1937. The success of this depended on pressure being placed on the General Post Office to establish the necessary communications network and on the RAF to structure and staff the organisation to which the Observer Corps was to report. It was under this new initiative that, in March 1936, Air Cdre A D Warrington-Morris was appointed as the new Commandant of the Observer Corps, taking over from Air Cdre Masterman who retired after seven years as its commanding officer. Despite severe financial restraints in the acquisition of sites and the building of Observer Corps posts, Warrington-Morris pressed ahead to meet the scheduled deadline. In July 1936 work on the expansion of the Corps was advanced enough for a combined conference to be held between the Air Ministry, the Air Raid Precautions Department and the GPO. This conference looked in detail at the extension of the Air Intelligence network and discussed a practical system of providing air-raid warnings for industry as well as for the civil population, taking into account the rapidly increasing speed and range of aircraft.

The impending threat to national security in Europe took a turn for the worse with the German repudiation of the Locarno Treaty (signed by Germany in 1925 to guarantee the then existing Franco-Belgian German frontiers), and the reoccupation of the Rhineland by German troops on 7th March 1936. Growing fears of a forthcoming major war in Europe were further reinforced by the outbreak of a civil war in Spain during the first week of July. The Air Ministry, aware of the growing numbers of Germany's front-line bomber aircraft and detecting an involvement of the Luftwaffe with Spain's Fascist forces, revived the whole question of the scale of Britain's anti-aircraft defences. No longer was an adequate early warning system enough, now specific plans had to be made for the protection of vital buildings, installations and resources. This necessarily involved the RAF, the Army and the Observer Corps and exerted an additional strain on an already taut programme of recruitment and training, as well as on the production of new equipment. The Air Ministry, conscious that the RAF was still a 'biplane air force', was applying pressure on the aircraft manufacturers to complete development programmes on prototypes that had evolved from design requirements issued back in 1934. As for the new generation of high-performance, eight-gun fighters, essential to the ADGB plans, the fabric covered Hawker F.36/34 (Hurricane) and the all-metal Supermarine F.37/34 (yet to be named the Spitfire) had both made their debut by March 1936. Of the two, the Supermarine was undoubtedly the better aircraft but, with its complex metal monocoque construction, it presented massive production problems when compared with the Hurricane's own

A specially commissioned portrait of Air Commodore A D Warrington-Morris CMG OBE (appointed as Commandant of the Observer Corps in 1936 to push through its dramatic expansion) painted by Oswald Birley in 1942.

conventional tubular steel and wood assembly. Proving tests, it was believed, had shown that both prototype aircraft matched Germany's latest development in fighter design, the Messerschmitt Bf 109. This pleased the Air Ministry because, even though the two British aircraft were well in advance of the original stated specifications, it meant there was great scope for further performance. Nevertheless, pressure to get both fighters into early production was unrelenting, and targets for the RAF to receive delivery to the designated squadrons by mid-1937 remained firmly in place.

Although the Air Ministry anticipated that detailed knowledge of Britain's fighter aircraft developments would eventually be appropriated by German Intelligence, Radio-Location, which promised to be an all-important aspect of ADGB planning, remained a closely guarded secret. It was barely a year old in concept, dating back to the first experiment on 26th February 1935, when Dr R A Watson Watt and his staff of three, in their small caravan close to the BBC's transmitters at Daventry, first watched the movement of a 'blip' projected in a cathode ray tube. They had fired off a 10kW signal, produced from the

BBC short-wave overseas transmitter, which was then deflected back to them by a Handley Page Heyford bomber flying along a pre-set track. With great foresight the Air Staff immediately allocated a budget for further work and a site at Orfordness on the Suffolk coast was acquired as an experimental establishment. Design work on the powerful transmitters and receiving aerials that would be needed to turn Radio-Location into a practical reality continued apace. By the middle of 1935 Watson Watt was able to report that an aircraft had been successfully detected and followed for some 40 miles. And in September he demonstrated the detection of an aircraft flying at a 15 mile range and at a height

the Observer Corps took place over the summer months. These were designed to test the various aspects of the defence of Britain and provided valuable training as well as an opportunity to analyse strategy. Plans for the September Air Exercises were modified, albeit secretly, to include the first real opportunity of testing Radio-Location in practice. The results gave great credence to a proposal for a chain of Radio-Location stations such as Bawdsey Manor and top priority was given to the establishment of five stations to cover the Thames Estuary, transmitting from Bawdsey in the north to Dover in the south. These stations were targeted to be ready by early 1937, by which time the RAF

The Radio-Location station at RAF Poling during the 1940s (a former AMES) showing the familiar cluster of three wooden masts between which was strung the Radio-Location transmission aerial.

of 7,000 feet with its altitude above mean sea level accurately predicted. In early 1936 the volume of work had outgrown the premises and a new experimental establishment was opened at Bawdsey Manor, just south of Orfordness. Watson Watt's team, fuelled by enthusiasm and support from the Air Ministry, increased their momentum and March saw the erection of the first 250-foot high receiving tower. This new structure finally proved the system and was able to track accurately an aircraft flying 75 miles away at a constant height of 1,500 feet.

During 1936 a series of combined military exercises involving the RAF, the Army, the Navy and

would provide suitable personnel for training as operators and technicians before placing the establishments under RAF/Air Ministry control. To consolidate all the results from the various areas of expansion and development in home defences, the Home Defence Committee of the War Office appointed a sub-committee under the chairmanship of Air Marshal Sir Hugh Dowding, C-in-C of the newly created Fighter Command (July 1936). His brief was to make recommendations as to the ideal structure for the air defence of Britain regardless of cost or current availability of equipment. The report of the sub-committee, which was largely uncritical but pressed for much more of the same and in a shorter timespan, was placed before the Committee of Imperial Defence in February 1937. This resulted in a proposal being put forward to extend the Radio-Location chain by a further 15 establishments to give cover from Portsmouth in the south, right along the Channel and up the east coast to the Firth of Forth in the north. That the pattern of coverage by these proposed Radio-Location establishments carefully followed that laid down for the expansion of the Observer Corps was no mere coincidence. But the Observer Corps was kept in complete ignorance of all these developments and the sites were designated as Air Ministry Experimental Stations (AMES), with a purpose, it was

Despite all the committees, all the reports and all the developments that had taken place over such a short period, 1937 failed to fulfil any of the targets that had been set. Problems with acquisition of suitable sites and delays with equipment supply hindered the setting up of the five new Radio-Location establishments; by late summer only three out of the five were operational. Development and production problems, not just with the airframes but also with the new Rolls-Royce Merlin engines, set back considerably the delivery of both the Hurricane and the Spitfire. And, although the expansion of the Observer Corps remained on schedule, its newly-recruited personnel had to rely on theory

A Messerschmitt Bf 109 B of the German 'Volunteer' (Legion Condor) Fighter Unit J/88 attached to Franco's Nationalist Forces and based at El Burga de Osma on the Spanish northern front.

rumoured, being to keep in long-range contact with the RAF bomber forces. Such rumours were deliberately fostered by the Intelligence Services, and endorsed by the leakage of titbits of supposed technical information. This was designed to add a misleading credibility to any reports on AMES that Germany might be receiving from its agents in Britain. The high level of secrecy was reinforced by the confident belief that Radio-Location was unique to Britain. Its 'non-existence', however, benefited the Observer Corps since they were now presented, both in Parliament and to the public, as Britain's front-line early warning system against attack from the air.

and 'synthetic' training. Since their value lay in a fast and accurate interpretation of the information obtained, this cast severe doubts on their abilities in a fully operational capacity. To add to Britain's problems by mid-1937 the Luftwaffe (under the guise of the 'Legion Condor' on behalf of the Fascist forces in the Spanish Civil War) was flying 24 production Messerschmitt Bf 109 Bs. Spain was an ideal testing ground for training and developing both men and machines (fighters, bombers, dive-bombers and others). Luftwaffe personnel were 'volunteered' for a specific tour of duty in order that as many pilots and groundstaff as possible gained from the experience.

The Observer Corps image of a post observer 'always vigilant and staring skyward with his binoculars while dressed in a rain cape and a tin helmet' was established during the mid-1930s.

In Britain the Air Exercises of August 1937 did little to relieve the pressure, with the three operational Radio-Location stations reporting many setbacks due to failures with their technical equipment. Nonetheless, the stations were able to prove successful plotting of aircraft movements at a range of 100 miles and up to 10,000 feet, and assurances were given that the technical problems were simple to resolve. That same month Treasury approval was finally given for the expenditure required to set up the next 15 AMES. And in mid-December, Dowding (now Air Chief Marshal) was relieved to see the first Hurricanes delivered to No 111 Squadron at Northolt.

The threat of a war in Europe precipitated by Germany moved one step closer to reality on 12th March 1938 when Hitler, assured by his rapidly growing military might, decided to break the clause in the Treaty of Versailles forbidding union between Germany and Austria. Assuming supreme command of his armed forces, he dispatched troops directly to Vienna and, aided by the lack of opposition, assumed control of Austria (Anschluss). The move was greeted by the new Prime Minister, Neville Chamberlain (the Conservative successor to Baldwin in an ongoing Government of National Coalition), with the pragmatic statement: 'Nothing could have arrested this action unless we used force to prevent it.' Despite this attitude of reluctance, which received support from those who believed that Germany had no interest in extending its territories into France or Britain, the fact remained that with Hitler's troops on the Italian frontier, Czechoslovakia was now exposed to a German advance from Austria. Suddenly it was the Sudetenland, a large Germanic province of Czechoslovakia and one time part of Austria, which Germany looked set to claim. Pressed on the Government's policy Chamberlain was forced to admit that: 'If Britain's ally, France, goes to the defence of Czechoslovakia, then Britain might apply "sanctions" on Germany in order to assist.' Little or no mention was made of Germany's current involvement in the Spanish Civil War, although in Britain the Chiefs of Staff were forced to accept the headstart of experience it was giving the German military, both on the ground and in the air. It was against this background of national upheavals and uncertainty that the first of Britain's 1938 series of combined military exercises, with their

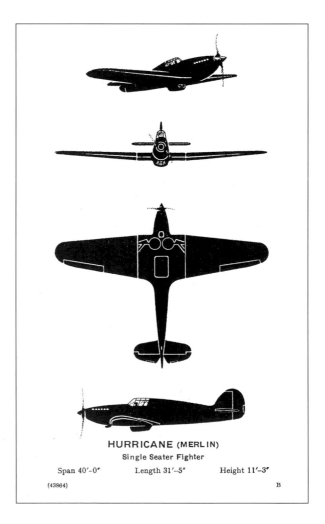

HURRICANE (MERLIN)
Single Seater Fighter

Span 40'-0"   Length 31'-5"   Height 11'-3"

(43864)   B

By 1938 the A.P.1480 silhouettes were simplified and revised for clarity but were not necessarily drawn more accurately.

heightened emphasis on home defence, was conducted in the Eastern Approaches to the Channel at the end of March. Criticism of Britain's defences against attack from the air was voiced in the House of Commons during May, in particular the fact that by the previous month only 28 Hurricanes were in service with the RAF (nearly two years later than targeted) and as yet there was no definitive date for delivery of the Spitfire. Viscount Swinton, the Secretary-of-State for Air, berated for his ministry's 'apparent' inability to cope, brushed aside the attack pointing out that this was merely the public and visible side of Britain's air defences: 'But the developing situation in Europe was giving them [Members of the Air Council] cause for great concern.' However, by August 1938 five Radio-Location stations were fully operational and the expansion of the Observer Corps was running to schedule. More anti-aircraft sites were being added according to a modified plan and the initial complex network of communications and control centres was in place and on 'standby'. To further confound the Air Ministry's critics, the first production Spitfires were being delivered to No 19 Squadron at Duxford. And, as had been the case in 1918 with Ashmore's LADA, the new defence structure, albeit in reduced form, was now ready for a full-scale test.

In less than a month the Munich crisis unfolded. From mid-August German military manoeuvres had been taking place on the Czech border and on 10th September Germany prohibited all flying over the Rhineland except in special air corridors. On 15th September Chamberlain flew to Munich for a conciliatory meeting with Hitler who was by now demanding immediate annexation of the Sudetenland, claiming its 'German' peoples were being subjected to anti-German harassment by the rest of Czechoslovakia. Returning to Britain the following day, Chamberlain entered discussions with his Cabinet; here he was joined by the Prime Minister of France, Edouard Daladier, and the French Foreign Minister. The idea was to sue for peace by agreeing to extensive cession of Sudetenland territory and to force the arrangement upon President Edvard Benes, the voice of the Czechoslovak Government. On 22nd September Chamberlain flew to Cologne to present the plan for partition, only to be met by Hitler's demands for immediate military occupation of a far greater area and an outright refusal of international supervision for its takeover. Back in London on 24th September a disillusioned Chamberlain was forced to declare: 'All concerned will continue their efforts to solve the Czechoslovakian problem peacefully.' There was

A WAAF Radio-Location operator tracks signals bounced off approaching aircraft on the cathode tube.

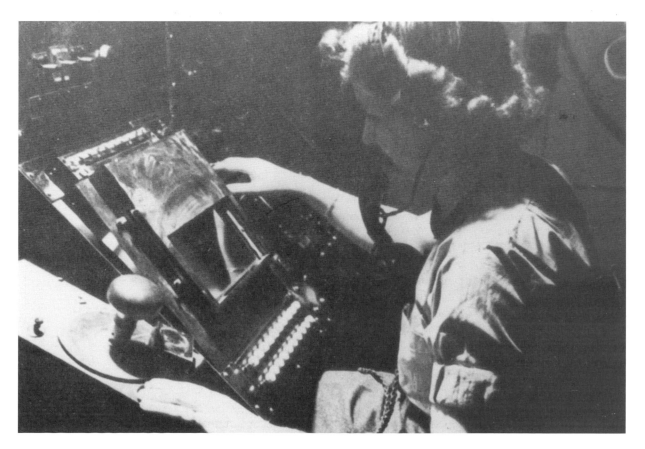

little doubt now that Britain was on the verge of war. The King signed a State of Emergency, certain branches of the Armed Services were mobilised, trenches were dug in the London parks, the evacuation of children from the capital was commenced and hospitals in target cities were readied to receive an onslaught of casualties. Information from the five operational Radio-Location stations, which had been carefully monitoring long-range aircraft movements since the announcement of 'no fly' zones over Germany, was now added to local information from a 'Called Out' Observer Corps and filtered to present a total picture of air activity both 'friendly' and threatening. Chamberlain next sent a message to Hitler appealing for a peaceful solution, in response to which he was invited by Germany's Fuehrer to attend a conference in Munich together with Daladier and Mussolini, Italy's Fascist dictator. At 8.30am on 29th September 1938 Chamberlain flew out to Munich and opened discussions with Daladier and Mussolini. Later that day they conferred with Hitler and by midnight had conceded to all his territorial demands but with international supervision. Before departing from Munich the following morning, Chamberlain issued as a press statement the content of a declaration signed jointly by himself and Hitler which was 'Symbolic of the desire of our two peoples never to go to war with one another again.' It was this piece of paper that he waved from the doorway of the British Airways Lockheed 14 at Heston Airport that afternoon. Chamberlain then immediately drove to Buckingham Palace to make his report to the King, after which he delivered the notorious 'Peace in our time' speech from the steps of No 10 Downing Street. On the 1st of October the House of Commons, by 366 to 144 against, ratified the Munich Agreement but with many Conservative abstentions by those wishing to dissociate themselves from Chamberlain. The

Neville Chamberlain at London's Heston Airport, on his return after signing the Munich Agreement.

The inside of the Receiver Block, which was the critical nerve centre of every Radio-Location stations.

First Lord of the Admiralty resigned in protest and Clement Attlee stated that, 'A gallant and democratic people have been betrayed and handed over to a ruthless despotism.' Those branches of the Armed Services that had been mobilised against attack were stood down and the Observer Corps returned to its part-time status. The only exception being the Radio-Location stations who continued to monitor long-range aircraft movements, supplying their information to the Air Intelligence branch of the Air Ministry.

The seven critical days of the Munich crisis provided much information on which the Chiefs of Staff could act. At the Air Ministry, unlike the Admiralty, there was a sense of relief at Chamberlain's achievement for the RAF was still ill- equipped to repulse an aerial attack. The idea that Britain might be involved in a European war had now taken on an air of certainty. Reliable intelligence sources were already advising on Hitler's next move and the Air Ministry knew it had to make best possible use of the time available, particularly with the supply of aircraft and the training of personnel. Testing of the organisation for defence against aerial attack proved that the system of identifying and reporting aircraft worked reasonably well. It had demonstrated the ability to operate with sufficient speed both for advanced air-raid precautions to be taken and for defensive fighters to be 'scram-

bled' and positioned ready to intercept enemy raiders. It had also thrown up minor technical faults and flaws in the system which would be remedied in the following months. Breadth of cover by the Radio-Location stations was now the principal worry. Although Treasury approval for the further 15 stations had been given in 1937, and sites selected, the Air Ministry was encountering tremendous delays in negotiating the necessary land sales. As a result of the Munich crisis these negotiations were immediately dropped in favour of compulsory purchase orders and mobile Radio-Location units were temporarily installed at the vital positions of Canewdon in Suffolk and Dover in Kent. Work on the construction of the buildings and the production of masts and equipment was speeded up and a new target date of the 1st of April 1939 set for the remaining stations to be operational. The role of the Observer Corps during the crisis, together with that of the Auxiliary Air Force (AAF), was roundly praised by Sir Kingsley Wood, the new Secretary-of-State for Air. Largely, the Observer Corps had encountered few problems with a full 'Call-Out', except for the need for extra headquarters and area headquarters staff to cope with the administrative requirements of a fully manned Corps. One anomalous problem was the ongoing part-time volunteer status of Observer Corps personnel. Still officially police specials, they had to be compensated for loss of their normal earnings during a call-out and thought had to be given by the Air Ministry as to what should happen in the event of a permanent call-out for war service. After the emergency the formation of further Observer Corps Groups continued as planned with the full complement anticipated to be in place by mid-1939.

The Air Ministry, via Air Intelligence (AI), had built up a fairly accurate picture of the Luftwaffe based on studies of German factories, shift work, raw materials and internal aircraft movements. Given this information it was able to approximate the German monthly output of aircraft and predict the size of the Luftwaffe in comparison to the RAF. The Air Ministry also had a specific interest in discovering the characteristics of the different aircraft types being produced, but unreliable intelligence in this area failed to establish many details of known aircraft in 1939 and useful photographs or drawings were almost impossible to come by. Studies of the Luftwaffe's 'Legion Condor' still fighting in the waning Spanish Civil War, provided little information except on the new, higher-performance Messerschmitt Bf 109 E that arrived to aid Franco in February 1939. Given the paucity of information available the question of aircraft recognition, which still remained outside the Observer Corps brief, continued as a low priority except for the Army's Anti-Aircraft (AA) Command who received updates of AP.1480 to

A copy of AP.1764 with [below] one of its pages.

ensure that they did not fire at 'friendly' aircraft.

Some thought was given to the problems of aircraft recognition by pilots and air gunners, and a sturdy pocket-size book, AP.1764, was produced for them to study. This was edited down to those aircraft types aircrews might reasonably be expected to encounter, both friendly and enemy, in the area in which they were to be operating. The enemy types, often lacking any real technical information, were drawn as halftone artist's impressions by a special department, AI.(a), set up in Air Intelligence and largely staffed by civilians. They also had the task of redrawing the silhouettes of British aircraft for AP.1480 from

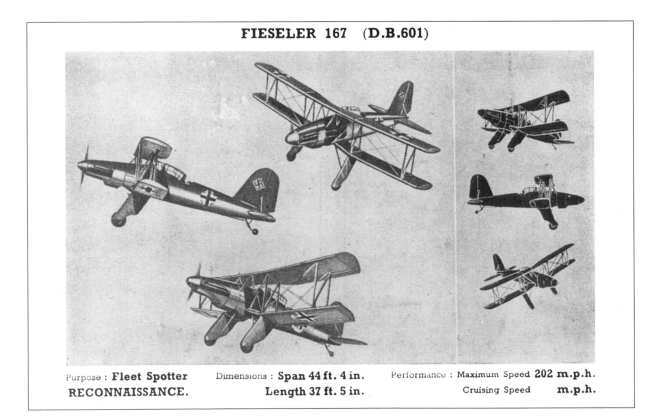

FIESELER 167 (**D.B.601**)

| Purpose : **Fleet Spotter** RECONNAISSANCE. | Dimensions : **Span 44 ft. 4 in.** **Length 37 ft. 5 in.** | Performance : Maximum Speed **202 m.p.h.** Cruising Speed **m.p.h.** |

the manufacturers' supplied plans or, sometimes with first prototypes, from their own sketched studies of the aircraft.

On 15th March 1939, as the Spanish Civil War came to an end, Hitler predictably invaded Czechoslovakia and established control in Prague. By now France, Belgium, Holland and Denmark had fully mobilised their armed forces and were regularly flying reconnaissance patrols along their respective borders with Germany. Suddenly the picture of aircraft movements in Europe became very confused with each country racing to get its latest types in the air and on operational service. Britain, still convinced that a German attack must come as a bomber offensive (intelligence studies had shown no evidence of production of the large bomber aircraft that would be necessary to make this strategy effective) concentrated on home defence. Intelligence had, following Hitler's demands for a corridor to the 'Germanic' free port of Danzig, predicted a German invasion of Poland in the autumn. This was undoubtedly the reason that August was selected for the next round of air exercises to be staged in collaboration with the French Armée de l'Air. Not only would a display of strength calm the fears of the British public but it would also demonstrate to Hitler the degree of Britain's readiness, in the certain knowledge that German agents would be scrutinising the effectiveness of the defences. In the first stage some 1,300 RAF aircraft, 53,000 men, 4 anti-aircraft divisions, 15

Observer Corps Groups, 700 searchlights and 100 barrage balloons took part in a first full test of the air and ground defences of the south-east of England. Aided by long-range detection from a dozen or more of the still highly-secret Radio-Location stations, now linked by a coastal hand-over to the Observer Corps, Air Chief Marshal Sir Hugh Dowding at Fighter Command Headquarters directed operations. Waves of bombers, sometimes protected by fighters, came from positions over 150 miles out over the North Sea to attack military targets only to find themselves successfully intercepted by the defenders. Impromptu attacks were flown by day and night, and in severely deteriorating weather conditions. Here lay the ultimate test for Radio-Location, for even a blinded Observer Corps was able to take over the projected radio-location tracks by detecting sound, and nearly every attack was intercepted. In the second stage of the Air Exercises seven Wings of Bombers, fighters and reconnaissance aircraft of the French Armée de l'Air flew over Britain as raiders. 'Attacks' were made on Manchester, Liverpool, other northern towns, and industrial areas in the Midlands and the West Country. All were successfully intercepted despite the fact that most of Britain's defences were concentrated in the south-east. A final French 'raid' was made on London with their fighter-escorted bombers flying low to avoid detection. This ploy, however, failed and squadrons of Hurricanes, Spitfires and Blenheim fighters intercepted the French over Surrey,

An Army gun crew on exercise demonstrate their expertise in handling the mobile 40mm Bofors anti-aircraft gun.

Sussex and Kent. An official communiqué after the Air Exercises were over, announced: 'These manoeuvres form a contribution to air co-operation between France and Britain which each day becomes closer and more efficacious.' At the same time the French High Command was seeking assurances from Britain that no less than six squadrons of RAF fighters would be dispatched to France the moment war broke out.

Within two weeks of the completion of the Air Exercises, Hitler made his next move and on 23rd August, to the astonishment of the rest of the world, signed a Non-Aggression Pact with the Soviet Union. By now German troops were massing on the Polish borders and the following day an Emergency Powers Bill was enacted by Parliament. This mobilised all the Service reserves, called-up volunteer forces, alerted the Air Raid Precautions network (ARP) and transferred control of Observer Corps personnel from the Home Office to the Air Ministry. Hitler, uncertain of Britain's position on Poland, summoned the British Ambassador in Berlin to pledge his Reich's support for the British Empire. That same day Chamberlain signed an Anglo-Polish Alliance, reaffirming an earlier agreement between the two countries. France immediately followed suit, Daladier making a public announcement that the French people would continue to uphold their pledges to Poland. The British Cabinet then sent a carefully

Neville Chamberlain seated at the desk in No 10 Downing Street from which he solemnly broadcast the 'Declaration of War' against Germany.

worded message to Hitler stating an interest in safeguarding Poland's essential interests and opening a wider understanding between Germany and Britain. On 29th August Germany announced that it was prepared to strike a deal with Poland provided that the proposals on offer were met in full. These proposals were then sent to Warsaw, but without waiting for a reply, Hitler ordered an invasion of Poland to begin at dawn on the 1st of September. Complete mobilisation of Britain's Armed Services was ordered and a second evacuation from London, this time of mothers and small children, began. The British Cabinet issued a warning to Hitler that unless his troops were immediately withdrawn Britain would stand by its obligations to Poland and oppose German aggression with force. By dawn on 3rd September, there had been no response to this demand and an ultimatum was issued stating that if a satisfactory reply had not been received by 11am that morning then a State of War would exist between Britain and Germany. At 11.15am a despondent Chamberlain broadcast to the nation from the Cabinet Room at No 10 Downing Street. Following a brief explanation of the situation and the action that had been taken he declared: 'I have to tell you that no such undertaking has been received, and consequently this country is at war with Germany.' Just 10 minutes after the broadcast the air-raid sirens began to wail across London. In fact it was a French Bloch 220 twin-engine transport bringing staff officers to an urgent meeting in the capital; it had been correctly identified as an intruder but unrecognised as a 'friendly' aircraft.

'THE BATTLE OF BARKING CREEK'

At approximately 0615 on the morning of 6th September, just three days into the war, a searchlight battery on the Essex coast reported a high-altitude formation of aircraft over Mersea Island heading towards the Thames Estuary. Their signal went to RAF Sector Operations at North Weald - where the unidentified aircraft were assumed to be hostile - and then on to No 11 Group Fighter Command HQ at Uxbridge and estimated positions for the raiders were set on both plotting tables. Since the raiders could possibly turn north, the Duty Controller of No 12 Group Fighter Command, based in Nottingham, was immediately informed, and the 'possible' raiders were plotted close to the Group's southern border. At 0618 the Sector Controller at North Weald, Gp Capt D F Lucking, contacted No 18 Group Observer Corps HQ at Colchester and advised them of the 'raiders'. The appropriate Radio-Location stations and the Observer Corps posts covering the area were at this stage unable to confirm the report of 'raiders' and this was advised to Sector Control. At 0630 No 11 Group scrambled one flight of Hurricanes (six aircraft) from No 56 Squadron from North Weald for a precautionary patrol at 11,000 feet between Harwich and Colchester. The squadron's commanding officer, Sqn Ldr E V Knowles, however, ignored the detail of the order and scrambled his complete squadron (12 aircraft). Imbued by the excitement of a full

squadron scramble, the two reserve pilots managed to get airborne in 'A' and 'B' Flights' reserve aircraft. Some five minutes behind the main squadron they flew to catch the formation and remained approximately half-a-mile behind and 1,000 feet below according to standard instructions for a 'maximum effort' scramble. At the same time as the scramble order was given to No 56 Squadron, Sector Controller again contacted No 18 Group Observer Corps to advise that six fighters had taken off on an easterly course to investigate. It was 0640 before Gp Capt Lucking realised that the whole of No 56 Squadron had been scrambled and even then he remained ignorant of the extra two aircraft. By that time reports from the Observer Corps posts were indicating the presence of a formation of unidentified aircraft at high altitude, positioned approximately along the projected track of the 'raiders'. Without waiting for confirmed sighting reports or to see how the track would develop, Lucking interpreted the presence of a full squadron 'up and searching' as vital and at 0645 ordered a further flight of Hurricanes from No 151 Squadron to scramble as a back-up patrol. At 0650 the Radio-Location station at Canewdon reported multiple plots of aircraft approaching the Thames Estuary from the east. This was the confirmation that No 11 Group Headquarters had been waiting for and at 0655 they ordered four flights of Spitfires (two flights from No 74

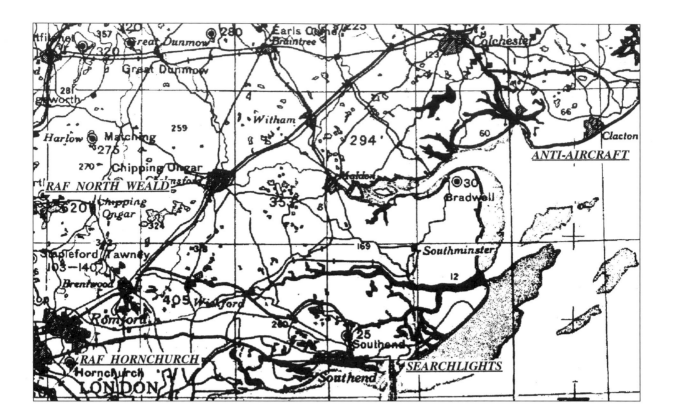

and one each from Nos 65 and 54 Squadrons) to be scrambled from Hornchurch and be vectored to intercept the 'raiders' at their operational altitude, which was greater than that of the Hurricanes.

A 'Red Alert' had now been declared in Greater London and the air-raid sirens were sounding throughout the area as well as in south Essex and north Kent. Within minutes an anti-aircraft battery near Clacton reported that it was firing at what it believed was 'a twin-engine aircraft presumed hostile'. Flying directly into the low angle of the early morning sun the two flights of No 74 Squadron Spitfires, who were the first to be airborne from Hornchurch, made visual contact with a large number of silhouetted aircraft and the 'A' Flight Leader called 'Bandits Ahead!' giving the approximate 'clock' position. One section of 'A' Flight, comprising Fg Off 'Paddy' Byrne, Fg Off John Freeborn and Sgt Plt Flinders, seeing shells bursting around two 'hostile' stragglers called 'Tally-ho!' and immediately dived their Spitfires into the attack, firing at and hitting two Hurricanes who were already suffering some ground fire. The pilots of No 56 Squadron immediately broke formation and scattered but the two Spitfires of Byrne and Freeborn pressed home their attack chasing their prey towards Ipswich. One Hurricane, flown by Plt Off Montagu Hulton-Harrop, was shot up and the pilot killed. The other Hurricane suffered substantial damage but its pilot, Plt Off

'Tommy' Rose managed to make a forced landing and escaped personal injury. The CO of No 151 Squadron, Sqn Ldr 'Teddy' Donaldson, whose flight of Hurricanes was rapidly closing on the affray, saw the potential for further disaster with 24 Spitfires locked into a dogfight with the remaining 18 Hurricanes and yelled: 'Do not retaliate. Bandits are Friendly!'. Concerned with all this activity close to his southern border the Duty Controller at No 12 Group in Nottingham decided to play safe and scrambled two full squadrons of Spitfires from Duxford (Nos 19 and 66). Fortunately this was a complete shambles, with dispersed aircraft facing each other at opposite ends of the airfield and, inadvertently, being ordered up at the same time (in the almost zero wind conditions that were prevailing this meant that they attempted to take off directly at one another). The result was that a milling crowd of 24 Spitfires was ordered back before they could further complicate matters. To add to the ignominy of the incident Nos 74, 65 and 54 Squadrons were subjected to intensive fire from the anti-aircraft batteries at Sheerness, Thameshaven and Chelmsford as they turned and presented their incoming silhouettes on recall to base. One Spitfire of No 65 Squadron was hit and damaged but its pilot was unhurt and all 24 aircraft finally landed safely at Hornchurch.

An immediate court of inquiry was convened and Fg Offs Byrne and Freeborn of No 74

Squadron were placed under arrest. Gp Capt Lucking, the Sector Controller was arrested on the orders of the AOC of No 11 Group, Air Vice-Marshal Keith Park, and taken to Group HQ under escort where he was advised he would stand trial by court-martial. In the event Byrne and Freeborn were acquitted of any blame but the full details of Lucking's court-martial, which may shed further light on the 'Battle', reside in a file in the Public Record Office stamped to remain closed. In its issue of 14th September 1939, *The Aeroplane* referred to a Ministry of Information bulletin on the incident which blandly stated that: 'Contact was not made with the enemy, who turned back before reaching the coast. On returning some of our aircraft were mistaken for enemy aircraft, which caused certain coastal batteries to open fire. This accounts for the rumours of heavy aerial engagement.' And: 'After being sent up to engage enemy aircraft the pilot of an RAF machine made a successful forced landing by the side of the road.' No mention was made of the fatality but *The Aeroplane* in its wisdom questioned the bulletin: 'The whole affair of this raid is very mysterious.' And, RAF Casualty List No 2 published on 25th September 1939, shows Plt Off M L Hulton-Harrop of No 56 Squadron as 'killed in action' 6th September 1939.

In all probability the original sighting by the over-anxious unit of the searchlight battery was that of a distant formation of duck or geese making their normal early morning passage from that night's roost in the Thames Estuary to a daytime feeding area. The Hurricanes sent to investigate would have been picked up by an operator at Canewdon Radio-Location station who possibly misread the plot and designated their track as its reciprocal. This 'mirror image' misreading of plots due to a 'technical malfunction' was not unknown in the early days of Radio-Location and would have had the unfortunate effect of confirming the searchlight battery sighting. Upon reaching the anticipated intercept position and finding nothing, the Hurricanes would have turned back only to present their incoming silhouettes to the expectant anti-aircraft batteries at Clacton. The three Spitfire pilots would then have seen, both ahead and below, a loose formation of incoming camouflaged aircraft being attacked by anti-aircraft fire. This was exactly what they expected to see and therefore moved to attack. The twin-engine 'hostile' shot at by anti-aircraft fire near Clacton was most probably a misread sighting of the silhouettes of the two No 56 Squadron stragglers flying as a close pair. And the opening up of the anti-aircraft batteries at Sheerness on the returning Hornchurch Spitfires was yet a further example of firing at what is expected to be seen rather than confirming the identity of the target first. A total embarrassment to all who were involved, the incident, in typical RAF black humour, was nicknamed the 'Battle of Barking Creek' after the main sewage outfall for Greater London at Barking close to where the offending Spitfire squadron was based. Officially brushed under the carpet as this tragic catalogue of errors was, it showed in a very poignant manner the need to establish some form of aircraft recognition training both on the ground and in the air. The Air Ministry, unfortunately, failed to comprehend this point of view and centred their blame on deficiencies in the telling, plotting and control organisation which was immediately modified.

A flight of Spitfire Mk Is answering the order to 'scramble' on an early September morning in 1939.

Members of the Observer Corps, although still only obliged to report four kinds of aircraft: 'Friendly Fighters', 'Bombers', 'Hostile' and 'Unidentified' (for the purpose of reporting all bombers were presumed to be hostile), had already been taking a lively interest in the subject of aircraft recognition. It added an extra dimension to their duties and they collected cigarette cards and photographs, made small solid-scale models and produced albums, selected by type, from various aircraft pictures that had appeared in print. They regularly bought copies of magazines like *The Aeroplane* and *Flight* (*The Aeroplane*'s long time rival), the former of which had recently published the first non-official identification book containing British, French and German aircraft with silhouettes and photographs. Among themselves Corps personnel

---

To
    Members of the Observer Corps
    living in the vicinity of
    GUILDFORD.

        It has been suggested that a study circle, or Club, should be formed in Guildford to provide facilities for members of the Corps to make themselves proficient in the practice of detecting, plotting and identifying aircraft.

        It is further suggested that the Club should meet at regular intervals and that its activities should include -

        (i)   the collection of large scale photographs
        (ii)   the collection of scale models of aircraft
        (iii) the collection of gramophone records of
                  engine sounds.
        (iv)   papers and addresses.

        In order to discuss the suggestions more fully a meeting will be held on

                SATURDAY, 9th DECEMBER 1939
                            at
            THE CORONA CAFE, HIGH STREET, GUILDFORD
                            at
                         2.30 p.m.
            (Tea will be served at 4 p.m., after which the
                    meeting will close)

        The speaker on this occasion will be PETER MASEFIELD of "The Aeroplane", and his subject will be

        "The Recognition of Aircraft".

        If you are interested in the formation of a Club as outlined in this notice will you please do your very best to attend the inaugural meeting.

Enquiries should be addressed to:-

        H. James Lowings, 34, High Street, Guildford.

                    Tel. 150.

THE HEARKERS' CLUB

Peter Masefield, technical editor of The Aeroplane and champion of aircraft recognition.

were already practising recognition abilities and some posts were producing daily log sheets of types of aircraft sighted. Despite a complete lack of official interest there was a belief among observers that it was in the long-term interests of both the Observer Corps and the Air Ministry that something should be done about formal recognition training. The first move was made in December 1939 by the members of No 2 Group based around Guildford, Surrey, who called a meeting of interested observers at the Corona Café in Guildford High Street. Peter Masefield, then technical editor of *The Aeroplane* and responsible for its early work on aircraft identification, was approached and invited to give a lecture on 'The Recognition of Aircraft'. Under the chairmanship of H James Lowings a first-ever recognition test was staged using 34 six-inch-square photographs of various aircraft in difficult attitudes taken by Charles A Sims for the *The Aeroplane*. Attended by some 40 observers the meeting was a resounding success (two observers, Douglas Jenkins and Peter Brooks, scored 100% in the test) and it was decided to formalise the idea into 'The Hearkers Club' with Lowings as Organising Secretary and Masefield as one of its patrons. This was a watershed for aircraft recognition and from monthly meetings in Guildford the club devised elementary, intermediate and advanced recognition tests that called for weekly meetings of 'The Hearkers School of Instruction'. Impressed not only by the club's rapid progress but also by the quality of its work, Peter Masefield revealed its existence to the public with a full-page article in *The*

Aeroplane. This resulted in a mass of correspondence from all over the world on the subject of aircraft recognition, some from would-be members of 'The Hearkers Club' who were not part of the Observer Corps. It was, however, decided that the club should remain exclusive to the Observer Corps and by the spring of 1940 it was producing its own journal *The Hearkers Club Bulletin* and had expanded to a further eight branches. Even where Observer Corps Groups had not formed their own 'Hearkers' branch, individual observers would make great efforts to attend the courses in aircraft recognition offered by the nearest branch, and to obtain one of the

'Before this war began nobody had realised the difficulties involved in the positive identification of British and foreign aeroplanes by ground observers, anti-aircraft gun crews, members of the Observer Corps and other defence forces. Most of the personnel of these essential defence units were not familiar with even our own most used aeroplanes. Thus the need for information on aircraft recognition became urgent. Now that British and German aeroplanes are seen over this country in a constant succession accuracy in identification is more important than ever'.

highly-prized, proficiency certificates which was the only way to become an official member.

In that same month, December 1939, Masefield, while still in full and active support of the newly-formed Hearkers Club at Guildford, launched his own public campaign for aircraft recognition training through the pages of *The Aeroplane*. Unlike officialdom, who throughout the 1930s had steadfastly ignored the importance of the subject, Peter Masefield was aware of the long-forgotten lessons of the last war with Germany and knew that this initiative was already late in the day. In an opening statement, on 22nd December, he reiterated the vital importance of positive identification of British and foreign aircraft by Britain's defence forces and therefore the urgent need for more information on aircraft recognition. More importantly, he

impression is the thing that counts, one knows one's father from his general appearance, not his detailed peculiarities although the small details are well known and go to form a composite picture which affords the instant recognition from any angle. The position is just the same with aeroplanes. When a type is really familiar it can be recognised at once by its general "sit" in the air. Little details, an underslung motor, a rounded wingtip, the position of the tailplane, all merge to form one complete whole which is perfectly distinctive.' Peter Masefield went on to state that familiarity could only come as the result of considerable study of detail and that to promote discussion and research on the subject *The Aeroplane*, in addition to the rudimentary silhouettes that it had been publishing, would regularly feature two aircraft recognition photographs showing details from British, German

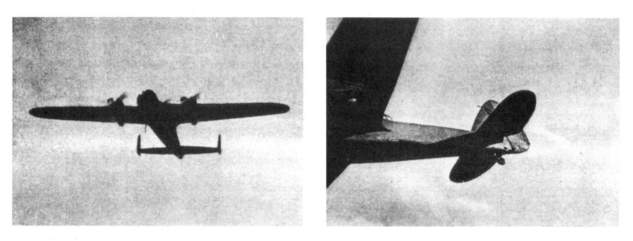

FOR IDENTIFICATION — The first of a series of photographs of Allied and German aeroplanes which we intend to publish for identification. What these aeroplanes are and notes on their recognition will be published with two more photographs next week.

moved on to discuss technique in aircraft recognition training, pointing out that to the untrained eye all monoplanes, high-, mid- or low-wing, looked much the same when flying at 10,000 feet and seen at a distance of some miles: 'Different people, new to the game, are adopting various methods to try to spot particular types of aeroplanes at a distance. Some look for distinctive features, such as motors, wings, tails, gun turrets and so on in a certain order and identify by a process of elimination. This method is excellent for a start, but is far too slow, laborious and meticulous to be of much use at the distance and speed at which positive identification will be vitally necessary when the real offensive begins. A useful analogy is that of meeting a stranger for the first time. He may be recognised next time by individual peculiarities, such as bushy eyebrows or prominent teeth. The general

and French aircraft with identifying marks painted out. The correct answers to those 'posers' were published the following week with some descriptive comment on the respective aircraft and both Masefield and *The Aeroplane* received much praise for seizing the initiative and putting a much needed momentum behind the subject. By February 1940 *The Aeroplane* had expanded its coverage with the first of a new series of whole pages devoted to the identification of British and German aircraft. These were something of a breakthrough with their clarity of features, comprising a main picture surrounded by 10 or more illustrations of the aircraft in various angles of flight and reversed (white on black) 5-position silhouettes with detail carefully line drawn in black. Lacking many suitable photographs from which to work the artist, Harold Bubb, made good use of the standard models produced by W G Woodason of Heston for the Air Ministry. And indeed, *The Aeroplane*, always anxious to produce the best very often pho-tographed these models for its 'Recognition' feature and for the revised editions of its *Aircraft Identification* books.

IDENTIFICATION OF GERMAN AIRCRAFT

I.—The Heinkel He 111K Mk. V$_A$ Bomber

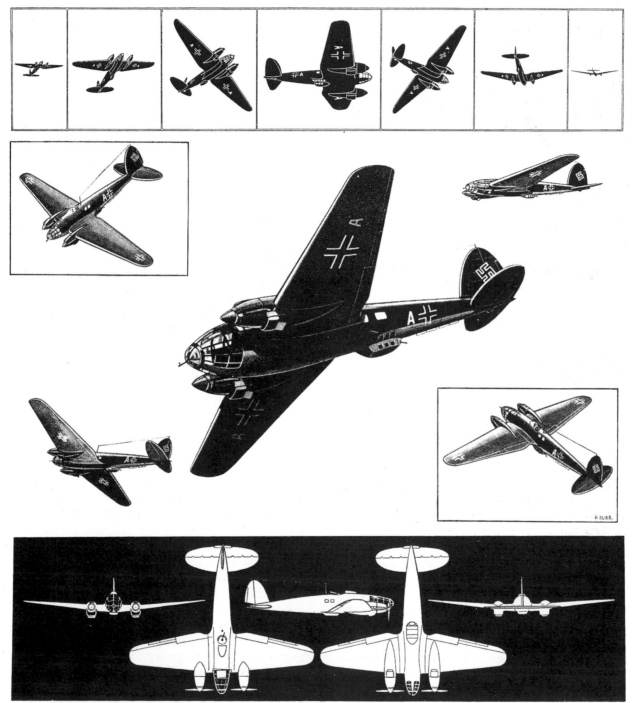

A GERMAN LONG-RANGE BOMBER.—The Heinkel He 111K Mk. V$_A$ (two Junkers Jumo 211$_A$ 12-cylinder inverted Vee motors; 1,200 h.p. each for take-off. Two-speed superchargers. Rated at 940 h.p. each at 13,800 ft.). All-metal stressed-skin construction. Crew, four. Colour, upper surfaces and sides black, under surfaces grey-blue. Span, 74 ft. 3 in.; length, 60 ft. 0 in.; height, 13 ft. 9 in.; wing area, 942 sq. ft.; empty weight, 14,100 lb.; max. overload weight, 27,400 lb.; max. speed, 274 m.p.h. at 12,300 ft.; max. overload range, 2,640 miles at 225 m.p.h. at 13,800 ft. Duration, 12 hours. Initial climb, 890 ft. per min. Service ceiling, 26,200 ft.

The mounting of drawings on sticks, held some distance away, was one technique for learning !

In late 1939 the Army was in much the same position as the Observer Corps regarding aircraft recognition. In the Army's case, however, batteries were not just advising on identity but were obliged to make for themselves the decision 'Friend or Foe' in the short time available before opening fire. The anti-aircraft and searchlight batteries all had aircraft spotters with a simple requirement to be able to report the direction of an aircraft aided by a pair of binoculars. Each battery was, however, required to fill out a 'Daily Report' of aircraft movements over its sector and this form specifically requested 'aircraft type'. To aid this form filling, and as a point of interest in their work, many of the battery NCOs made reference to books of cigarette cards and whatever illustrated material they could lay their hands on (copies of AP.1480 although distributed to AA Command were thin on the ground). This was less than satisfactory and the Royal Artillery, prompted by the Chiefs of Staff after a plethora of complaints by the RAF that their aircraft were being fired at, decided to set up a training scheme in the Anti-Aircraft Command. The plan was to form an Aircraft Recognition Wing under Capt R D Linton at the RAF station, Biggin Hill. Linton was to structure and run courses for officers and senior NCOs both in the subject itself and in its instruction for their respective units. With no aircraft recognition precedent from which to draw guidelines (there was an Inter-Service Recognition Committee, formed in mid-1939, but it was primarily concerned with pyrotechnic and light signals from aircraft to ground or sea forces to reveal their identity), the establishment of the Wing was obliged to start from scratch with little knowledge of where to begin. One of the instructors, Cpl Leslie Whitfield, was posted

from a searchlight battery because he was reported to have performed well with the 'Daily Report'. Ill-equipped as they were, a team of four rapidly produced a syllabus, a system of examination and grading, read just about anything that had been written on aircraft recognition techniques and gathered as much training equipment as they could get their hands on. Whitfield remembers: 'The supply of aircraft models was totally inadequate, a number of 1/72 models of British aircraft - mostly biplanes and about ten 1/36 models of German aircraft. The Air Ministry had granted the munificent sum of five pounds for the purchase of items not available through official channels. This money quickly disappeared in the acquisition of 1/72 'Penguin' plastic moulding kits of the Spitfire, Hurricane, Lysander, Miles Magister and others. Even so the Wing was still very short of models of important aircraft and all four of us were frantically engaged during every spare moment in making models from balsa wood based on the photographs we had been supplied and the silhouettes in AP.1480. Soon we had a good display in the classroom spread over tables on each side of the platform - about 35 Allied (mostly British) and 25 Axis (mostly German).' Examination papers were prepared, projector slides obtained and suitable accommodation organised on the RAF station. Capt Linton knew that for the first few months they would often be only one-step ahead of those they were teaching but he had developed great confidence in his small team and he knew that if he could prove the Wing a success he would achieve the backing that it deserved. By 12th February 1940 the Wing was officially open and without due ceremony welcomed its first 36 students from AA Command to the ten days of 'Course No 1'.

As 1940 developed both the Observer Corps 'Hearkers School of Instruction' and the Anti-Aircraft Command 'Aircraft Recognition Wing' grew from strength to strength. A loose relationship was struck up between the two organisations but with the 'Phoney War' rapidly coming to an end, there was little opportunity for an exchange of ideas. On 9th April Germany invaded Norway and seized Denmark. An Anglo-French force was immediately dispatched to aid Norway's defence and by 19th April they were fighting the Germans at sea, on the land and in the air. The Allied response, although fierce, was rapidly overcome by the sheer weight of German numbers and on 2nd May it was all over; what was left of the Allied force was driven from the centre of Norway. Eight days later, on 10th May, Hitler invaded Luxembourg, Belgium and the Netherlands and began to pour thousands of troops into France. Germany's domino tactics were being repeated, only now Britain was one of the pieces. And, no longer was there room for a Government with a background of peace initiatives. With the full backing of the House of Commons a Wartime Coalition Government was immediately formed with Winston Churchill as Prime Minister. This was none too soon; by 21st May the German advance was closing on the French Channel ports and the British Expeditionary Force (BEF) was taking a beating.

The Air Ministry, worried about the very heavy losses being sustained by the RAF squadrons in France and about the supply of fighter aircraft needed to ensure Britain's defences were capable of meeting an all-out attack, spared little thought for anything else. Believing that such an attack was imminent, Dowding refused to release Spitfires to help in France, fearing their loss when they would soon be needed at home. The coastal 'Chain Home' (CH) Radio-Location stations were now fully operational and supplemented by a series of 'Chain Home Low' (CHL - AMES 2) Radio-Location stations that provided cover from the ground up to 1,000 feet, an area omitted by the long-range CH stations. The RAF Reporting and Control Network had also been further modified with information being carefully filtered and the decision-making removed from Sector Control to Group Control who worked in direct liaison with Fighter Command HQ. The work of the Observer Corps had become an intrinsic part of that reporting system and of particular importance in taking over hostile tracks reported by the Radio-Location stations. The instructions for aircraft recognition and reporting procedures for friendly aircraft remained the same as set in August 1939: 'To report all formations of 2 aircraft or more by day but to state if they can clearly be recognised to be friendly by one of the following

Anti-aircraft batteries were positioned all along the Channel coast as a first line of ground defence.

The scene at a typical town centre observation post in the south eastern sector between 1940-41.

Revisions were made to the Observer Corps plan to extend cover in the north and the south west.

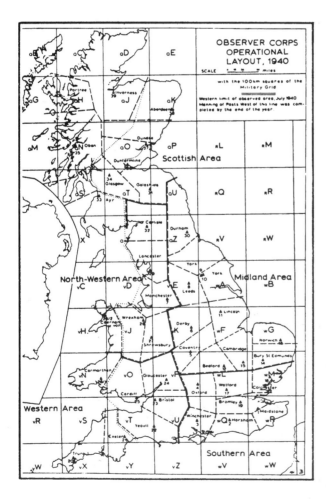

methods - (a) Aircraft flying in line astern. (b) Training aircraft, which will be coloured yellow. (c) Civil aircraft, which will be coloured silver and carry their normal civil registration letters. (d) Fighters, which will have their undersurfaces coloured black on the port side and white on the starboard side. (e) Aircraft flying with undercarriage lowered. (f) Biplanes. (g) Single-engined aircraft'. These instructions, with the 'safeguard' of coded visual signals which could be made by 'friendly' aircraft if under threat, were all that the Air Ministry and its sub-committees felt were necessary. There was, however, a growing mood of dissent among several senior RAF officers both in the commands and in the control centres. But, with the threat of a German attack now on the horizon, anything to do with aircraft recognition, despite its now more apparent merits, had to be pushed to one side for the interim.

Surrounded and forced back onto the beaches of Dunkerque, a rapid evacuation of the defeated BEF by 4th June was followed by the German occupation of Paris on 14th June and, on 22nd June, by the ignominious formation of a French government of the non-occupied zone based in Vichy and controlled directly by the Germans. Britain, although supported by the countries of the Commonwealth, now remained the only threat left to Hitler and the question was 'when' and not 'if' Germany would invade. Military Intelligence was well aware of Hitler's invasion plans, codenamed 'Sealion', of which the first objective was the destruction of the RAF. Also, they knew that Germany was busy preparing a long-range bombing force and they predicted that a sustained air offensive would begin around the first of July. The eyes, ears and radio waves of Britain's defences were concentrated across the Channel and out over the North Sea, straining to identify a change in the relatively small-scale bombing tactics so far employed by the Luftwaffe.

On 7th July, almost on schedule, the major offensive on Britain began with 75 air raids stretching from Dover to Falmouth. At first it was intensive attacks on shipping and ports but by the end of July the emphasis switched to RAF stations and aircraft factories. This continued, on a daily basis, for the whole of August and into September, a period during which every aspect of Britain's defences was stretched to its limit and beyond. However, despite German claims to

the contrary, the RAF failed to buckle under the pressure and its losses were almost evenly matched by those of the Luftwaffe. The supply of RAF fighters, now under the Ministry of Aircraft Production, continued largely uninterrupted due to the programme of 'shadow factories' which separated production from assembly and spread it variously around the country. For the moment the concentration of hostilities remained on military targets in the south and the work of the majority of those now committed to aircraft recognition was able to continue uninterrupted. An added advantage was that there were now many crashed and one or two flying examples of German aircraft available for official examination and study. However, under the pressure of work now placed on Observer Corps personnel, 'Hearkers Club' meetings suffered and the Army's Aircraft Recognition Wing was forced, by enemy action, to evacuate from Biggin Hill and found itself in various temporary locations during this period. The campaign, initi-

The Observer Corps centre of No 38 Group during 1940 with plotters and tellers in position around the main board, all wearing their lapel badges and the blue and white 'Police Special' armbands.

The Daily Mirror, ever keen to be topical, produced its own identification booklet in September 1940.

ated by *The Aeroplane*, which had now been taken up by many other publications, continued in the same format and in September the magazine published its first book of collected *Recognition Tests*. Daily newspapers, fully aware of the public interest in German aircraft, had also taken to publishing recognition silhouettes although many of these, like those in AP.1480, were of a poor quality. On 7th September, in a final effort to deplete the RAF's reserves, the Luftwaffe changed its tactics and started bombing Britain's principal cities, in particular London, but the tactic failed and the ratio of losses, RAF to Luftwaffe, remained the same. In truth the intensive bombing campaign had cost the Luftwaffe dearly and intelligence reports advised that by mid-September an enraged Hitler had been forced to concede the failure to destroy the RAF and had therefore ordered the invasion plan to be cancelled. This did not mean the Luftwaffe was going to cease its offensive but rather to redirect it. The substantial German aircraft losses in raids during the last week of September caused an immediate switch in policy. Emulating the RAF, the main weight of daylight raids were scrapped in favour of the intensive night-time bombing of Britain (the 'Blitz') which was to continue well into 1941.

By the end of October 1940, with the 'Battle of Britain' now successfully over and the Luftwaffe denied dominance of Britain's skies, there was an opportunity to evaluate the performance of Britain's defences for the period of the 114 days. Amid the air of both relief and self-congratulation that surrounded this appraisal there emerged one particularly damning statistic, namely that no fewer than 20 British front-line fighters, bombers and transports (mainly Spitfires, Hurricanes and Blenheims) had been shot down by British anti-aircraft fire and a further nine aircraft (mainly Blenheim twin-engine fighters and bombers) had been shot down by the RAF's own fighter pilots. Such information was, of course, suppressed, but the loss of over two squadrons of aircraft to 'friendly' fire could not be ignored. It was obvious to the Chiefs of Staff at both the Air Ministry and the War Office that the problem of aircraft recognition had to be addressed at a more serious level; the point being further reinforced by a letter passed to Sqn Ldr Newbiggin, Secretary of the Inter-Service Recognition Committee, for his immediate attention: 'My son received the Freedom of New Romney last Saturday (2nd November 1940) in honour of his winning the Victoria Cross and flew down from his base at Scampton for the ceremony. He came under hot fire from local machine-guns near here while he was circling round to let us know he was on his way and then flew off to Hawkinge where he was due to land. There they opened up properly on him, with fairly well directed anti-aircraft fire and finally he had to fly back to Manston. I fear it was partly Roderick's fault, as owing to flying around here first he approached Hawkinge from the wrong direction; but as they had been warned to expect him you could have thought that they would recognise a Hampden bomber flying fairly low and evidently wanting to land.' In fact Flt Lieut Roderick Learoyd VC finally landed at Manston with some 20 bullet and shrapnel holes in his No 49 Squadron Handley Page Hampden (which, with its twin tails, could just possibly have been mistaken for a Dornier Do 17) and with his friend, the second pilot, nursing a large shrapnel wound in one leg.

'At the sky we stare by day and night,
To identify and plot unwelcome guests,
And with each speck observed we ask,
Did we get that bloody aircraft right?'

Observer Corps anon - 1940

A NEW SENSE OF DIRECTION

Between mid-November 1940 and July 1941 continual and extensive raids were made by the Luftwaffe on nearly all the principal cities and towns of Britain, with London still bearing the brunt. Almost every night streams of German bombers crossed the English coast from as far west as Plymouth, right around the south and reaching up to the extreme north-east. Although the Battle of Britain was won, and the threat of an imminent invasion averted, Britain's defences were as stretched as ever. Throughout this period the major German air raids constituted 200-700 bombers reaching the target with smaller scale raids of 20-80 bombers visiting other targets at the same time. In addition there were 'harassment' raids by small groups of bombers revisiting the scene of a major attack night after night, in an effort to prevent a return to normality. Further attacks were made on coastal targets and shipping, often in daylight and with the support of fighters, in an effort to blockade Britain's vital supply links. The prelude to this was the raid on the city of Coventry during the night of 14/15th November 1940 when between 7.20pm and 3.50am a force of 449 German bombers, out of an initial 509, dropped 495 tons of high explosive and 3,200 incendiaries on the city - killing 568 people, seriously injuring 863 others and devastating the whole of the central area. This policy grew out of Hitler's belief that intensive bombing would reduce the will of the people to fight and therefore either force Churchill into submission or enable the Germans to launch a revised invasion plan. The RAF, however, was doing its best with an expanding Bomber Command to hit back at Germany and Churchill, still in buoyant mood from the success of the Battle of Britain, was not ready to submit to anything. This was the period during which the newspapers declared 'Britain can take it' and, backed by Air Intelligence projections that Germany's bombing initiative would eventually run out of steam, the War Cabinet continued to plan ahead.

Although there was a mass of aerial activity over Britain's night skies, both the Air Ministry and the War Office had gained a significant advantage through accurate advanced knowledge of when and where the German raids were going to take place. At the highest possible level of secrecy, the Combined Intelligence Services (Navy, Army and Air Force) had been working since 1939 to intercept German wireless traffic and to crack the codes used for all levels of communication by the German Armed Services. These codes were changed daily using a complex mechanical computer called 'The Enigma Machine' and cracking the code meant logging thousands of messages, attempting to decrypt them, translating the results from German to English and analysing them to make sense of the information. By May 1940 the 'Enigma Red Key', which was the root from which to decode the transmissions of the German Air Force, had been cracked. It was, however, of little tactical use during the Battle of Britain because of the time taken between decrypting transmissions and translation into perfect 'intelligence'. Also there was a necessary period of learning for analysts to understand the workings of the Luftwaffe and, therefore, how to interpret this information. During the summer of 1940 the majority of the intercepts were for signals of high- and medium-levels of importance. As Autumn approached the regular interception of German low-grade signals (Sigint) was achieved and this helped considerably by supplying much needed detail of the Luftwaffe's intentions and movements. Such was the case that by the time of the raid on Coventry (German codename 'Moonlight Sonata') both the Air Ministry and the War Office knew most of the details, except the exact target. Birmingham was the other major possibility and at 3.00pm the RAF's No 80 Wing (Radio-Counter-Measures) at Radlett reported the detection of two German navigation beams crossing-over in the Midlands. At the same time an 'Enigma' coded message, confirming Coventry, was decrypted and the respective Chiefs of Staff immediately informed of what to expect. (The X and Y Verfahren precision bombing system of transmitted beams had just been introduced by the Luftwaffe to aid night- and blind-flying accuracy on the target). The fact that only a moderate effort was made to intercept the streams of German bombers *en route* to Coventry (effectively a squadron of aircraft every 10 minutes over an eight-hour period) was as much due to the RAF's shortage of night-fighters as to a policy of sacrificing Coventry to avoid revealing that 'Enigma' had been cracked. Although official records show that operational limitations were no less important than security problems in maximising operational use of the information obtained, the intelligence provided an invaluable supplement to early warning Radio-Location plots. Supplied to only two senior officers at Fighter Command, the intelligence was filtered and leaked in various ways (covering its sources) so that it could be used by the RAF, the Army's AA Command and also the Civil Defence Services, who were sometimes able to dispatch reinforcements to a target before the German bombers arrived.

A scene of total devastation in the centre of Coventry after the intense air-raid of 14th November 1940.

Despite the Air Ministry's Radio-Location service and the Observer Corps remaining in complete ignorance of the work of the Combined Intelligence Services, the successful analyses and use of the Luftwaffe's 'Enigma' coded communications had a great significance on high-level policy thinking with regard to both. Neither organisation was now expected to be searching in a void but to confirm intelligence reports and add accurate updates once a planned raid was on its way. This did not always hold true as the analysis of decrypted information was by no means guaranteed to be accurate but it did now seem to make sense to extend the Observer Corps duties and to take aircraft recognition seriously. This would have the combined effect of helping to reduce the incidence of damaging losses of the RAF's own aircraft to 'friendly fire' as well as to aid Air Intelligence analyses by reporting accurately on types and variations of

points of view on aircraft recognition were discussed at length. The RAF, represented by its three front-line Commands, and Home Forces favoured the idea of creating a national training centre. Lieut-Gen Sir Frederick Pile, C-in-C of AA Command, reported on the achievements of the AA Aircraft Recognition Wing which was producing about 120 instructors a month. The Admiralty representatives, headed by Capt E Longley-Cook, concluded that, despite Fleet Air Arm interests, the Admiralty was unable to support the formation of a committee to co-ordinate training in aircraft recognition. In his view: 'The existing 12,000-yard Fleet Artillery Zone surrounding all HM Ships at sea [in which all aircraft would be fired at] remained adequate and therefore there was no necessity for sending personnel to a recognition centre for instruction.' The Admiralty would, however; 'Take all possible steps to improve Naval proficiency in aircraft

Right - Lieut-Gen Sir Frederick Pile, C-in-C of AA Command and one of the most influential members of the Inter-Service Recognition Committee.
Left - Air Marshal Sir Philip Joubert de la Ferte, Chairman of the Inter-Service Recognition Committee and its most senior RAF representative.

type of enemy aircraft as well as any other anomalies that might be visually observed. By the end of 1940 the Observer Corps 'Hearkers Club' had managed to develop, quite independently of the Army's Aircraft Recognition Wing, an ideal programme of recognition training complete with proficiency tests which was both ready and easy to absorb into the officialdom of the Air Ministry. The decision of January 1941 to make the 'Hearkers Club' an 'official organisation', place the Commandant of the Observer Corps at its head and to change its name to the Observer Corps Club, came hot on the heels of the eighth meeting of the Inter-Service Recognition Committee. This meeting was significant because, even though the Observer Corps was not represented, the agenda addressed the subject of formal aircraft recognition training for the first time. Under the chairmanship of Air Marshal Sir P B Joubert de la Ferte the differing

recognition.' Faced with the Navy's intransigence and the already acknowledged success of the Army's 'school', Joubert de la Ferte was forced to accept that training had to be the responsibility of the individual Services. As far as the RAF was concerned this placed the matter firmly with the Directorate of Technical Training. The question of the Fighter, Bomber and Coastal Commands running their own aircraft recognition units was raised but this was discounted and Air Cdre M Thomas, Director of Technical Training, together with Gp Capt R Nelson, were asked to come up with a solution. This resulted in the formation of an RAF Aircraft Recognition Sub-Committee under the Synthetic Training Committee. Its brief was simple: 'To establish, with all possible speed, an aircraft recognition Wing which, like the Army's, would produce Instructors who could be deployed throughout the Commands.'

Registered at the G.P.O. as a Newspaper.

THE AEROPLANE SPOTTER

Proprietors:
TEMPLE PRESS LTD.

Managing Director:
ROLAND E. DANGERFIELD

Head Office:
BOWLING GREEN LANE,
LONDON, E.C.1

Telephone: TERminus 3636

**Incorporating
The Bulletin of the Royal Observer Corps Club**
Edited by PETER G. MASEFIELD
M.A. (Eng.) Cantab; A.F.R.Ae.S.
Technical Editor of "THE AEROPLANE."

FOR THE ALERT

THURSDAYS

3D

OF ALL NEWSAGENTS
OR DIRECT FROM THE
PUBLISHERS, POSTAGE PAID

12 Months 17/4 6 Months 8/8 3 Months 4/4

Almost in parallel with Air Ministry and RAF concern about aircraft recognition training, Peter Masefield was campaigning with the directors of Temple Press, publishers of *The Aeroplane*, to produce a separate weekly publication devoted entirely to the subject. The object being, using the exceptional facilities enjoyed by the parent magazine, to broaden material so far published by supplementing it with articles, illustrations and cutaways, to aid a detailed understanding of the many different types of aircraft and their technical constructions. Called *The Aeroplane Spotter* and incorporating *The Hearkers Club Bulletin* its imminent publication was hurriedly announced in the 27th December 1940 issue of *The Aeroplane*. In the opening statement of the first issue, dated 2nd January 1941, its Editor, Peter Masefield, wrote: 'The need for such a news sheet has been expressed partly in the vast-ly increased sales of *The Aeroplane* arising from its special services in identification matters, and partly in the demand by those in the RAF, in the anti-aircraft batteries, in searchlight crews, as well as in the Navy, the Mercantile Marine, the Army and the Home Guard, the Observer Corps, the Balloon Barrage and among the "Jim Crows" or roof watchers, for full, regular and accurate information in words, photographs and silhouettes on the identification of aircraft.' He went on to state that: 'Accuracy is the first essential in work of the type which this new publication sets out to perform. The demand for material on aircraft recognition has become so great within recent months that a flood of hastily prepared and dismally inaccurate information has been sent out from many quarters not closely in touch with aeronautical matters.' The first 8-page issue of *The Aeroplane Spotter*, although somewhat

THE NEW MESSERSCHMITT.—The first Messerschmitt Me 109F2 to be forced down, almost intact, on British soil. Noteworthy points are the new and rounded spinner, the rounded wing tips and the new cantilever tailplane. The armament is one 15 mm. cannon firing through the airscrew hub and two machine-guns on the cowling. The top speed is about 380 m.p.h. at 21,000 feet. In action it has proved inferior to the Spitfire and Hurricane.

unsophisticated in comparison with later issues, was an immediate sell out and sackfuls of congratulatory correspondence began to arrive at the offices of Temple Press. Within a month of its publication it received official recognition from the Air Ministry and the War Office, who placed orders for subscriptions for all RAF stations and AA Command units, and the Observer Corps Club made it their official journal. A unique publication, printed in-house on newsprint that had been gleaned by reducing pages in several of the other Temple Press journals, it set a three-day copy date which allowed for a vital immediacy in its content.

Mid-January 1941 marked the start of the RAF's new aircraft recognition initiative which was to be quite apart from the air intelligence requirements of the Air Ministry and therefore not part of the Observer Corps' own training scheme. Some fundamental aircraft recognition, 'air-to-air', was already being taught at the RAF Initial Training Wings but little of the knowledge either remained or was of use by the time aircrew were posted to operational squadrons. Although aircraft recognition material (including *Flight* magazine's famous large-scale poster) was evident in all aircrew rooms, there was no curriculum for any regular recognition training and no regime for updated information. The need was to establish a 'school' which would produce instructors

who, based at a squadron or a wing, could provide both basic and refresher courses relevant to the theatre of war in which the aircrew would be operational. Initiated by the Aircraft Recognition Sub-Committee, the plan was to establish a 'school' attached to the RAF Gunnery School at Ronaldsway on the Isle of Man. Flt Lieut V L Barrow from Technical Training Command, who already had some experience with aircraft identification, was selected to head the 'school' and, swallowing a modicum of RAF pride, potential NCOs were booked into Instructor Courses Nos 26 and 27 at the Army's AA Command Aircraft Recognition Wing. Leslie Whitfield remembers: 'The first group of eight were absolutely hopeless - and Capt Linton reported back to the RAF stressing the importance of careful selection of students. The second group were no better and as a result the RAF sent a Flt Lieut (Admin) with four sergeants on Course 28 to find out what was going wrong. The Flt Lieut was graded as barely acceptable and two of the sergeants as possibles. Not much with which to handle 50 students on a new subject in five days time.' Flt Lieut Barrow realised he had a problem, the first course was set to begin at the end of February; so, completely swallowing RAF pride, he asked the Army for their direct assistance. The result was that 2nd Lieut Emmanuel and (now) Sgt Whitfield were seconded for six weeks to the RAF to use their expertise in organising, lectur-

The Army and the RAF working together on silhouette sheets to improve their aircraft recognition skills.

Leading Aircraftmen study the various elements of aircraft recognition training in the principal 'recognition' room at the RAF's newly established school at the 'Villa Marina', Douglas, Isle of Man.

ing and helping to establish the 'school' at the 'Villa Marina' in Douglas (a large building with a ballroom which had been acquired for the purpose). The first RAF Recognition Training Wing course commenced on 26th February 1941 and followed the same syllabus as the Army's. Initially all the lectures were delivered by the seconded Army personnel with those RAF NCOs trained at the AA Command 'Recognition

School' taking part under supervision. Several promising students from the first courses were retained to gain more experience in the hope they would qualify as permanent school instructors. Among these was one, ex-commercial artist and established caricaturist, Cpl E A 'Chris' Wren who was starting to contribute his famous 'Oddentification' drawings to both *The Aeroplane* and *The Aeroplane Spotter.*

Beaufighter Mk IIFs of No 406 Sqn RCAF, in special night finish and fitted with MK IV AI sets.

While visual identification and recognition were being addressed seriously, and Air Intelligence together with Radio-Location was providing the vital long-range early warning of impending raids by the Luftwaffe, there remained a large hole in Britain's defences against attack by night. During the early months of the Blitz, despite knowing the exact radio beams that the Luftwaffe would be using to navigate, both AA Command and the RAF's night-fighters were literally stabbing in the dark with scant results. Blind at night, the Observer Corps was entirely dependent on sound tracking which was not accurate enough for systematic interception. Searchlight units and anti-aircraft units were reduced to using antiquated sound-locators for elevation and track. And, the RAF's few trained night-fighters were worse than useless unless they could be vectored into an extremely close visual range. The solution, it had been known for a long time, lay in the development of small, portable short-range radio-location equipment that could be carried in night-fighting aircraft or appended to AA guns and searchlights. However, all development in radio-location had been given over to the vital CH and CHL networks and work on other radio-location projects had been forced to wait. By the latter half of 1940 night fighting had become a priority and while the Battle of Britain was raging in the south, Bawdsey Manor was working flat out with radio equipment manufacturers to produce sets which could be operational by early 1941. 'AI'

sets (Air Interception) were first tried in fighter aircraft in late 1939 but it was not until the autumn of 1940, with the production of the MK IV version fitted as a test into a twin-engine Beaufighter, that an effective system was achieved. This now gave the pilot and his operator a blind detection scope of nearly 4 miles and a minimum of 600 feet and this set remained free of the malfunctions that had plagued earlier versions. 'GL' (Gun Laying) and 'SLC' (Search Light Control) radio-location installations for the Army followed much the same pattern of problems and progress.

Again it was the autumn of 1940 before the first MK I GL installations were supplied to AA Command and there were far too few of them to meet the requirement of one installation per 4-gun unit. In addition they were imprecise, giving a range of 40,000 feet but with a height accuracy only within 1,000 feet and directional bearings that wandered at elevation angles over 45 degrees. This was less than satisfactory but for the interim it was considered better to aim at the supposed position of a target than to fire wildly into the night. As with 'AI', development pressed ahead and by the spring of 1941 a 'serviceable' version was put into use which gave the AA guns accurate information on the target's height, range and bearing. At the same time a smaller scale transportable radio-location unit, named 'Elsie' and produced for Search Light Control, made it its appearance.

With the mass of radio beams thrown up to locate and identify raiding German aircraft, and without the possibility of accurate visual recognition at night, it would have been only too easy to confuse the RAF's own aircraft activity with that of the enemy. The solution to this problem, which had been devised but not developed in late 1939, was the 'I.F.F.'(Identification Friend or Foe) apparatus to be carried by aircraft. This was simply a small receiving and transmitting set which received 25 megacycle pulses from ground radio-location stations or installations and replied with a coded pulse on the same wavelength. Although the wavelength remained constant the coding, which was numeric and therefore offered countless thousands of possibilities, could be changed as and when required. The set, when switched on, would only be triggered to transmit by receiving the correct pulse which would then be shown on a radio-location operator's cathode ray tube as a pulsing blip or 'pipsqueak'. Without this device it would have been impossible to identify accurately the hundreds of RAF bombers that were flying every night to targets over Germany and returning, some badly damaged or short of fuel. It also would have been impossible to identify single night-fighters which, together with the development of the 'GL' radio-location installations, gave Sir Hugh Dowding and his staff at Fighter Command an idea.

The concept was 'GCI' (Ground Controlled Interception) in which a controller using a localised network of GL installations would be able to vector, via a radio link, a night-fighter directly onto its target by observing his coded IFF 'pipsqueak' in relation to the 'enemy' blips and position him close enough for his 'AI' to be effective. It also had the advantage of being able to identify the enemy for the night-fighter, removing the still necessary, and difficult, visual recognition before the pilot opened fire. The first experiments were conducted with MK I GL installations diverted from the Army's AA Command. A series of 10 were located at a number of selected searchlight sites in the Kenley Sector and linked by landline to the Sector Operations room. There, the radio-location plots on enemy raiders were updated every 30 seconds providing a constantly changing but accurate picture of the aerial activity in the night sky. The experiment was considered a success and development was immediately commenced on the production of specially designed GCI units which, unlike the limited GL installations, would have a range of 50 miles. These were to be strategically positioned on an overlapping grid covering all possible paths taken by German

raiders as well as around sensitive target areas. In early 1941 the first fully trained night-fighter pilots were emerging from the RAF Operational Training Units, Beaufighters were starting to be produced in numbers and the first of the very rapidly developed GCI units were being put into operation. By the spring of 1941 Britain was no longer in the dark, technology had won the battle for location, identification and recognition of the enemy at night. It was these major achievements in the use of the radio-wave that was to spell a dramatic change in the fortunes of the Luftwaffe.

One of the GL gun-directing radio-location sets used by Dowding for his GCI chain experiment.

On 9th April 1941 the Secretary-of-State for Air, Sir Archibald Sinclair, in answer to a prepared question in the House of Commons, announced:

'I am happy to inform the House that, in recognition of the valuable services rendered by the Observer Corps over a number of years, His Majesty the King has been graciously pleased to approve that the corps shall henceforward be known by the style and description of The Royal Observer Corps.' This long sought after recognition, finally pushed into place by the Air Ministry, marked a significant change in the status of the Corps. First of all Controllers and Assistant Controllers were given officer ranks, the Observer Corps Club albeit officially recognised was now to be termed 'Royal' and given direct financial assistance, and plans were made for a uniform for the ranks of the 'R.O.C.'. The duties of the Royal Observer Corps were more closely defined, attention being paid to their future position in the defence strategy especially in relation to the growing Radio-Location network. Sensibly, the Air Ministry decided that reliance on technology alone (the development of an inland Radio-Location network using GCI installations to replace the Corps) would make Britain's defences too vulnerable to an attack either by ground or by air: 'The Royal Observer Corps must remain fully manned and fully trained, especially in aircraft recognition where it offers the only visual confirmation available, and

Despite cramped confines, home comforts were not ignored by observers inside their ROC field posts.

to continue to plot and report aircraft movements with the very considerable accuracy it has managed to achieve.' Also the technology was not as reliable as many people had been led to believe and continuous tracking overland remained the prime responsibility of the ROC. Another important aspect was the filtering of erroneous 'blips' on the radio-location tube which did not give rise to defensive action. These were often caused by 'friendly' bombers, disabled aircraft, those that were lost and strayed and aircraft that had no business to be where they were located. There was, however, one other important function for the ROC that had been brought about by the demonstrable inadequacies of the public air-raid warning system.

Considerable economic damage was being inflicted on Britain, both in war production and general manufacturing, during air-raid warnings. Quite often, as was the case in the early days of the Blitz, German formations would pass nowhere near but, because of an air-raid warning, workers took to the shelters, production was halted and considerable time was lost. Worse still were the cases of single aircraft, which could be misidentified or were just on reconnaissance. Millions of man hours were being wasted and, in late 1940, the Ministry of Home Security tried to persuade workers to treat the air-raid siren as an 'Alert'. Official sanction was given to the idea of factory roof Raid Spotters, nicknamed 'Jim Crows', whose job it was to give the 'Alarm' when a raiding force was actually in sight. None of this was totally satisfactory and by November 1940 an official system of 'Alarm- within-the-Alert' instigated by the Observer Corps was first tried out. This required the appointment of an 'Alarm' Controller to the Group Centres who would be responsible for sending a 'Two-Minute' warning to selected factories and organisations of the approach of enemy aircraft. After a raid the 'Release' message would then be given providing there were no enemy aircraft remaining within a 30 mile radius of the factory concerned. This system worked well and underwent rapid expansion during the early months of 1941, large industrial companies having their own Control Point linked by landlines direct to ROC Group Centres. This also allowed the ROC Alarm Controller to advise the factory when 'friendly' aircraft were approaching so that no accidental 'Take Cover' warning was called. But there was still a time delay in these warnings and it was a Raid Spotter's job to recognise aircraft and to assess the situation, including aircraft position, closing speed and intent, and to reduce to a bare minimum the time given for an 'Alarm'. In the first instance Raid Spotters could have been anyone employed by a factory whose management felt might be more useful 'watching' than at a workbench. It was soon realised that an 'Alarm' which lasted for three minutes could cost 15-20 minutes production time as the workers also had to shut down and restart machinery. This amount of time lost, multiplied by several thousand in a workforce, meant that the Raid Spotter carried an enormous responsibility. Realising this, factory managements looked for advice to the Ministry of Home Security and were soon careful about the quality of their Raid Spotter teams. As private individuals the only formal aircraft recognition training available was as part of a Civil Defence Services 'Roof Watcher' course where the Chief Instructor, Mr S F Sabin, had established the WEFT System of recognition (Wings-Engines-Fuselage-Tail). There was, nevertheless, an ever growing number of books on the subject of aircraft recognition including two, *The Spotter's Handbook* and *Night and Fire Spotting*, both by Francis Chichester, which were published in early 1941 expressly for Raid Spotters.

The two books written by Francis Chichester (better known in later years as the single-handed round-the-world yachtsman) prior to him joining the RAFVR as a navigation officer.

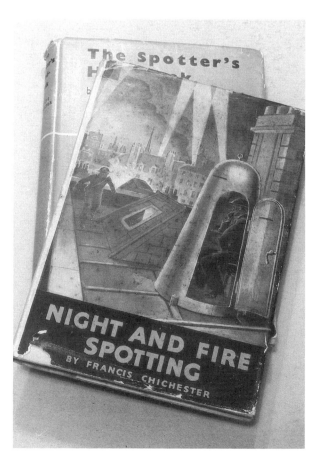

The original design for the badge of the National Association of Spotters' Clubs.

February 1941 also saw the start of the 'Spotters Clubs'. The first was formed at Southend-on-Sea by keen Raid Spotters and based on the original self-help ideals of 'The Hearkers Club'. A brief mention of this in the 6th February edition of *The Aeroplane Spotter* was all it took to start the ball rolling and new clubs began to form throughout Britain. Raid Spotters were not supplied with any official material and they had no easy way to update information. Neither was there any authority who could examine their proficiency and, although their work was considered invaluable, they received no national recognition. *The Aeroplane Spotter* by its very existence was the 'official' journal of the Raid Spotter, therefore its Editor was honour bound to champion their cause. This Peter Masefield did by encouraging the formation of Spotters Clubs centred around the 'art' of aircraft recognition rather than the specific role of the Raid Spotter. His reasoning was simple: there was a great deal of amateur interest in the subject particularly among Britain's youth and it would be from their ranks that future experts would be drawn.

By May 1941, aided by the *The Aeroplane Spotter*, 50 clubs were up and running on 'Hearker' principles and Peter Masefield masterminded a conference at the Royal Aeronautical Society's headquarters in London. This enabled the formation of a General Council of the 'Affiliated Spotters' Clubs' and an approved constitution which provided for co-operation with the ROC and ensured that: 'On the subject of

Aircraft Recognition, the two organisations shall go forward along parallel lines.' It set out a National basis of 12 areas, corresponding with the Civil Defence regions, each with its own council. Training was to follow the ROC pattern, complete with the same series of proficiency tests, and designs were submitted for a badge. Full membership was restricted to registered Raid Spotters, members of HM Forces and persons actively involved in the British aircraft industry and associate membership was open to all others. The appointment of Wg Cdr E J Hodsoll, the Inspector-General in Charge of Raid Spotting at the Ministry of Home Security, as the first President-General with H James Lowings, the Organising Secretary of the Royal Observer Corps Club, as a committee member guaranteed that the new organisation had official blessing. *The Aeroplane Spotter* expanded its size to create a regular whole-page feature devoted to the Affiliated Spotters' Clubs. The clubs were encouraged to retain their own identities and although the hardcore remained in the hands of the Raid Spotters, new spotters clubs were formed at schools, were allied to aircraft modelling clubs and were formed by squadrons of the Air Ministry's recently created Air Training Corps (formerly the Air Defence Cadet Corps of the Air League). The growth of the movement continued apace and by August 1941 some 150 clubs were fully affiliated enabling the name to be changed to 'The National Association of Spotters' Clubs' and an official badge issued for use by the full members.

The badge of the NASC, supplied as a transfer, which was worn on the tin helmets of 'official' Raid Spotters.

A miscellany of visual aircraft recognition training aids both military and civil, including posters, manuals, charts, playing cards and recognition models in wood, buckram and cardboard.

PLATE 7.

T is for a TERRIFYING TYPHOON.

THIS BRITISH SINGLE SEAT FIGHTER with a 2,400 h.p. Sabre motor can carry two 500 lb. bombs under the wings. A very fast climber with a top speed in the region of 400 m.p.h. Deep radiator under the short nose, broad wings and a straight back to its fin and rudder are its main features. Looks rather aggressive with its four cannons protruding from the wings.

Illustration from the *ABC of Aeroplane Spotting* by A R 'Lofty' Haynes (an instructor at the War Office School of Aircraft Recognition) published in early 1944.

PLATE 8.

At the beginning of 1940, when the Army's AA Command started its Aircraft Recognition Wing at Biggin Hill, there was a distinct shortage of material for teaching aids and much had to be improvised. Nearly 18 months later, with Hitler's attentions focused on the Russian front and the Blitz gradually petering out, the situation was reversed with an abundance of material now available, some of which was of extremely poor quality. Silhouettes were fundamental to teaching aircraft recognition and much controversy raged about their standards, their accuracy and their presentation to suit teaching methods. The Air Ministry's AP.1480 series of loose-leaf recognition books, first produced in 1934, had long been criticised for the inaccuracy of its drawings and steps were taken to rectify this. True silhouettes with thick white lines showing minimal detail were adopted together with silly ideas, such as spinning propellers and disproportionate pilots heads. These revised silhouettes still suffered from a great deal of criticism and two different schools of thought arose about the degree of detail that should be shown. One school advocated that silhouettes should be presented in the form that the aircraft would be most likely to be seen in the sky (completely black), while the other school believed that silhouettes were nothing more than a teaching aid and it was by the collection of details/features that an observer would learn to recognise an aircraft. These arguments came to the fore with the publication, in early 1941, of a Penguin Books paperback, *Aircraft Recognition*. Compiled by R A Saville-Sneath, it was criticised by Peter Masefield in *The Aeroplane Spotter* for its use of the official silhouettes. Particularly so, because Saville-Sneath was a contributor to the magazine and the policy of both *The Aeroplane* and *The Aeroplane Spotter* was to use medium and thin white lines to illustrate primary and secondary detail. Saville-Sneath immediately resigned from *The Aeroplane Spotter* and wrote a long letter decrying Peter Masefield's thinking. This was

Despite the adverse criticism Saville-Sneath's book sold some 7,000,000 copies to members of the less discerning public during World War II.

duly published and followed-up with an article illustrating the differences but reinforcing the teaching principle. The latter thinking was endorsed by the AA Command Aircraft Recognition Wing (now called the Anti-Aircraft Command Recognition School - AACRS), by the majority of the Observer Corps and by the RAF's 'school of aircraft recognition'. Even so the Air Ministry held back and it was not until the end of 1941 that the first official replacement silhouettes, suitably detailed with medium and thin white lines, began to be published.

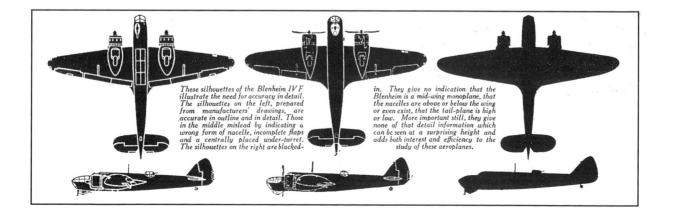

These silhouettes of the Blenheim IV F illustrate the need for accuracy in detail. The silhouettes on the left, prepared from manufacturers' drawings, are accurate in outline and in detail. Those in the middle mislead by indicating a wrong form of nacelle, incomplete flaps and a centrally placed under-turret. The silhouettes on the right are blacked-in. They give no indication that the Blenheim is a mid-wing monoplane, that the nacelles are above or below the wing or even exist, that the tail-plane is high or low. More important still, they give none of that detail information which can be seen at a surprising height and adds both interest and efficiency to the study of these aeroplanes.

Silhouettes were produced in many forms: From small poster sizes on newsprint to large-scale composite posters; in various shapes and formats as recognition handbooks; on transparent sheets of plastic for use at sea; in card sets for epidiascope projection, for speed testing and for proficiency grades; in a game called 'Sieg Heil'; and as playing cards, both as recognition games in their own right and later as informative decoration on the face-side of normal packs. The first playing card set, called 'War Planes', was produced by Temple Press in 1940. It consisted of 52 cards in which all side-views of the 13 aircraft featured were represented by Spades, all above-views Hearts, all below-views Diamonds and all end-views Clubs. In addition there were 13 general-view cards plus two special key cards. As well as conventional card games, the instructions for playing a special 'war game' were included. Simple silhouette playing cards were first supplied to RAF Recognition Instructors for use in the operational squadrons during 1942 and were produced by the Ministry of Aircraft Production (MAP). There were four packs with coloured backs: Red for single-engine, Blue multi-engine single-rudder, Orange multi-engine multi-rudder and Green miscellaneous aircraft. Each pack of 52 cards featured 18 aircraft (12 Allied and 6 Enemy) and instructions were issued for several games, based on conventional cards games, in which accurate recognition was essential in order to play.

Other vital aids to aircraft recognition teaching were models, photographs and films. Models were of prime importance not only for their versatility in teaching but, as with enemy aircraft, they were often the only subjects readily available for the camera. Made of wood, 'Bakelite' and a non-essential material called 'buckram', the recognition models were usually produced in 1/72 scale with far less detail than the established scale-model kits, and finished in either matt-black or matt-grey. The early versions, with moulds made from drawings supplied by Air Intelligence, like the silhouettes, were often inaccurate and much criticised. By late 1941 revised models were being produced based on drawings supplied by the aircraft manufacturers or, in the case of enemy aircraft, from drawings produced by AI.2(g) after detailed study of Intelligence photographs or the examination and measurement of crashed and captured examples. Models were in great demand (in mid-1941 contractual requirements amounted to 200,000 models) and, apart from the more obvious companies such as Lines Brothers (manufacturers of FROG and Penguin kits) who devoted a large part of their war production to the MAP, cabinet makers and boatbuilders such as Jack Holt were using their expertise to supply the Air Ministry's requirements. Models, especially for photogra-

JUNKERS Ju 88 A-4

HEINKEL He 111 H-1

Two of Woodason's models photographed for recognition training by K H Gaseltine of Ilford Ltd.

phy, were made by W G Woodason who also worked with K H Gaseltine (a member of the ROC) of Ilford Ltd to produce simulated in-flight photographs which were so good that it was nearly impossible to tell them from the real thing. Other photographs came direct from the manufacturers, from the Photographic Section of the Aeroplane and Armament Experimental Establishment (A&AEE) at Boscombe Down in Wiltshire and from *The Aeroplane* and *Flight*, whose acknowledged expertise in aerial photography was a sore point with several members of the RAF Aircraft Recognition Sub-Committee. Photographs, after being suitably retouched, were printed on cards or sheets and hundreds of thousands of them were distributed to those involved in aircraft recognition. Films were particularly significance to the RAF because of the the ability to show changing angles through movement. The first of these were primarily produced for aerial gunnery training and compiled from a mixture of footage mainly from the camera guns fitted to RAF fighters. These images were often out of focus and imbued with camera shake which considerably reduced their value for training. A special series of purpose-made recognition films featuring some 30 types of Allied and Enemy aircraft were commissioned by the MAP for use by the War Office and the Admiralty. They were produced by Analysis Films with the technical help of *The Aeroplane* under the direction of W M Larkins (an Observer Corps Group Officer who also worked at the J. Walter Thompson advertising agency). These featured models, together with some Paramount Newsreel footage, and used white line work superimposed on sections of the images to aid comprehension of the distinctive features. Larkins' films were well received as a step forward in recognition training, not least by the ROC and the AACRS. There were, however, senior RAF officers on the Aircraft Recognition Sub-Committee who disagreed. In a secret report dated April 1941 it was stated that such films were lacking in the realism required for RAF training and that recognition films should feature aircraft 'actually in flight'. The proposal was that the Photographic Section of the A&AEE should co-operate with Gaumont British or Pathe Gazette using an aeroplane from the Special Duties Flight at Boscombe Down as a camera platform. This attitude was at variance with other members of the Inter-Service Recognition Committee but they agreed that the RAF's requirement for 'air-to-air' recognition training differed from the 'ground-to-air' requirements of the other defence organisations. By way of a good British compromise it was proposed: 'Where possible, quality flying footage would help to enliven these films creating greater enthusiasm among the audiences.' Consequently, recommendations were made to investigate the establishment of a small film unit at Boscombe Down under Air Ministry control.

Another important consideration was the possible use of the number of German aircraft that had fallen into British hands since the beginning of the war. Various Luftwaffe aircraft had been brought down by the defences in a reasonable state of repair. Others had forced landed due to poor navigation, defection or simply run out of fuel and been secured before their pilots could set them ablaze. These aircraft had been collected by the Air Ministry and allocated to various research establishments and specialist units for Luftwaffe aircraft. These were flown for evaluation by such distinguished test pilots as Gp Capt H J Wilson and it was not uncommon for a dogfight between a Messerschmitt Bf 109 E and a Spitfire or a Hurricane to be seen in the air over Farnborough. Air Intelligence and the RAE were, however, principally interested in the latest German developments and as the supply of enemy aircraft grew there were many examples both flying and static that became surplus to its requirements. Some of the static examples were

'Messerschmitt earns cash for Spitfires' stated the London Evening News when this downed Bf 109 E was put on enclosed display in the East Croydon Station car park with an admission of 6d per person.

testing and evaluation. The principal benefactor was the Royal Aircraft Establishment (RAE) at Farnborough in Hampshire who used its expertise to create flying examples out of spare parts gleaned from other specimens. The aircraft were all given RAF serial numbers and over painted with RAF roundels and markings. Although the very first examples of crashed German aircraft had been the subject of much scrutiny by Air Intelligence specialists, by late 1941 the RAE possessed quite a few of the commoner passed to local and national authorities for exhibition to raise money for causes such as War Bonds and The Spitfire Fund but this still left several aircraft in perfect flying order. Mindful of its recent aircraft recognition initiative, the Air Ministry instructed the RAF to form a 'Captured Enemy Aircraft' flight. Whether or not this was a conscious resurrection of the successful 'Flying Circus' recognition activities of the First World War, No 1426 (Enemy Aircraft) Flight was formed at Duxford on 21st November

A captured Junkers Ju 88 A-5 that landed short on fuel, sustaining only minor damage, at RAF Chivenor after its German crew became lost, mistaking Cardigan for North Devon and the English Channel for the Bay of Biscay in November 1941. This proved ideal for the RAF's shortly to be formed Enemy Aircraft Flight and after repair it was flown to Duxford via RAE Farnborough in December.

1941 under the operational control of No 12 Group, Fighter Command. To be supplied by the RAE with enemy aircraft types as and when they became available it initially received two twin-engine bombers, a Heinkel He 111 and a Junkers Ju 88 A, and a Messerschmitt Bf 109 E fighter. The Flight boasted a full 'German' maintenance unit complete with spares and all its ground crews were specially trained by the RAE at Farnborough. Under the command of Fg Off R F Forbes, an established RAF test pilot, the Flight's brief was simple, 'To tour all operational RAF stations and display the Enemy Aircraft, in the air and on the ground, for the benefit of aircrew, ground staff and aerodrome defence personnel and to fly the Enemy Aircraft for fighter liaison and aircraft recognition duties.' This meant working with the newly established film unit at Boscombe Down and resulted in some of the first meaningful air-to-air footage of enemy aircraft to be incorporated into the 'new style' recognition films.

A captured Heinkel He 111 H-1 (originally designated a He 111K Mk Va) that became the first aircraft to be released by RAE Farnborough, from its growing stock of examples, to the RAF's Enemy Aircraft Flight at Duxford. This particular aeroplane was originally acquired by the RAF when it was forced downed by a Spitfire near North Berwick, Scotland in early 1940 and proved to be repairable.

The ROC had decided, in September 1941, that while retaining its association with *The Aeroplane Spotter* it would publish its own magazine. *The Journal of the Royal Observer Corps Club* was quite different from *The Aeroplane Spotter* in both standard and content, running to 36 pages of good quality reproduction every month. Only for sale to ROC members, it con-

centrated on the practicalities of teaching aircraft recognition, the ROC proficiency tests and other ROC functions. It also, following on from the examples of 'Chris' Wren, put a great emphasis on putting interest into the subject via humour and other devices. Humour as aid to teaching had already proved itself invaluable in various RAF and Air Ministry publications and it was this same indigenous service humour that ran through the pages of the *Journal of the Observer Corps Club*. With an editorial committee headed by Air Cdre H Le M Brock, which including H James Lowings, the *Journal* owed much to the commercial publications and was supported by Peter Masefield both by editorials in *The Aeroplane Spotter* and his own written contributions. Although well received by the Air Ministry, particularly for its style and content, it fell outside the area of 'Classified Material' which ruled out publishing articles on certain subjects which would have been of use to the

Teaser No 3 - Vultee Vengeance. Teaser No 4 - Tomahawk. Test No 1 - What are they: Bf 108 Aldon, Bf 109 F, Mentor and Airacobra.

TEASER No. 3. WHAT IS IT ?

FISH & POULTRY.

TEASER No. 4. WHAT AEROPLANE IS THIS ?

TEST No. 1. WHAT ARE THEY ?

ROC. This point was made by the Inter-Service Recognition Committee when it was charged by the Air Council in November 1941 to: 'Conduct an investigation into the state of aircraft recognition training and the methods of production and distribution of aircraft recognition material.' The problem was the lack of co-ordination and policy, with each Service going its own way and the production of material variously divided between official sources and the private sector. Admittedly, aircraft recognition had been a major growth industry since late 1940 with most of the initiatives coming from the commercial magazines. As satisfactory as that was in a time of great need, it no longer met with Air Ministry approval and pressure was applied to make material and teaching methods 'official'. Following the Japanese attack on Pearl Harbor in December 1941 the United States finally entered the war; this meant that by mid-1942 US Army Air Forces (USAAF) would be operating with the RAF. The arrival of American aircraft, plus their pilots and their air gunners, would considerably add to the problems of recognition training and procedures and this had to be considered by the Inter-Service Recognition Committee. The 'Report', which took detailed account of individual papers supplied by the three Services and other official bodies concerned with aircraft recognition, was not presented to the Air Council until March 1942. It attempted to be far-reaching and critical but, with the exception of a rationalisation of recognition material, it was forced to concede the impossibility of establishing one controlling body for aircraft recognition training. It therefore recommended the formation of a training sub-committee: 'To ensure where possible, Inter-Service co-ordination on organisation and methods of training.' This brief was also extended to include the Civil Defence Services. The substance of this report, fully endorsed by the Air Council, had an immediate effect on the RAF who, in April 1942, terminated its Aircraft Recognition Sub-Committee and created a new Visual Aircraft Recognition Training (VART) Committee. Chaired by Gp Capt H D O'Neill, Deputy Director of Operational Training, this new committee had a more vigorous policy for aircraft recognition training throughout the RAF, with direct control over the Recognition Training Wing at Ronaldsway and a voice on the inter-service committees.

At the same time the ROC was under scrutiny by the Air Ministry and a report into its future, which redefined the importance of an existing role in parallel with Radio-Location, advised that it should be run on strictly military lines.

Air Commodore G H Ambler RAF, appointed to Commandant of the Royal Observer Corps as part of the new initiative in June 1942.

This included training and advised that aircraft recognition tests, hitherto optional although taken by the majority of observers, should become mandatory with proficiency grades which would relate to rank and scales of pay. The first move was to change the Commandant of the Corps from a retired RAF officer to one currently serving and this meant the enforced retirement of Air Cdre Warrington-Morris and his replacement in June 1942 by Air Cdre G H Ambler. This was not well received by ROC members who had always been fiercely proud of the Corps' semi-amateur status. Worse still was the new compulsory retirement age of 50 and a general move to upgrade the standard of personnel. Instructions were issued that women observers, who had only been recently accepted into the Corps should be recruited to replace those men considered unfit for further service. There was resistance to this both from the Ministry of Labour and from the War Office who considered the ROC should be manned by 'low-grade' personnel. In a secret memo to the Assistant Chief of Air Staff, the Director of Fighter Operations, Air Cdre J Whitworth-Jones, made the point that with enemy interference of Radio-Location signals and the impending threat of low-flying attacks on specific military targets, it was of the greatest importance that the ROC was manned to the highest possible standard: 'We want women for their mobility and their intelligence. The latter quality is hardly to be expected in military throw-outs. Anyway, we have more than enough of low-grade manpower

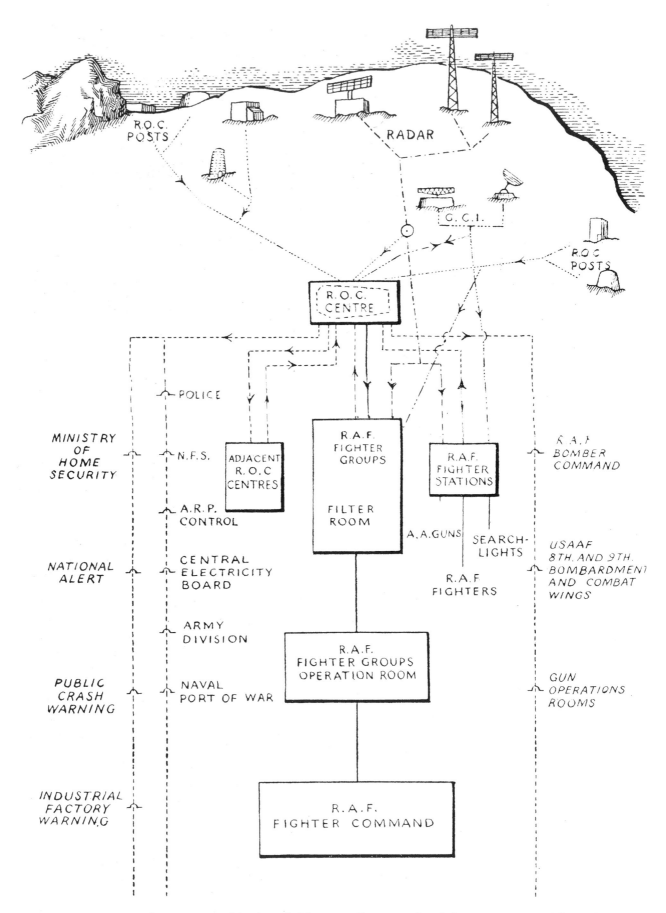

R.O.C.
POSTS

RADAR

G.C.I.

R.O.C
POSTS

R.O.C.
CENTRE

POLICE

MINISTRY
OF
HOME
SECURITY

N.F.S.

ADJACENT
R.O.C
CENTRES

R.A.F.
FIGHTER
GROUPS

FILTER
ROOM

R.A.F.
FIGHTER
STATIONS

R.A.F
BOMBER
COMMAND

A.R.P.
CONTROL

A.A.GUNS

SEARCH-
LIGHTS

NATIONAL
ALERT

CENTRAL
ELECTRICITY
BOARD

R.A.F
FIGHTERS

USAAF
8TH. AND 9TH.
BOMBARDMENT
AND COMBAT
WINGS

ARMY
DIVISION

PUBLIC
CRASH
WARNING

NAVAL
PORT OF WAR

R.A.F.
FIGHTER GROUPS
OPERATION ROOM

GUN
OPERATIONS
ROOMS

INDUSTRIAL
FACTORY
WARNING

R.A.F.
FIGHTER COMMAND

Diagram depicting the position of the Royal Observer Corps in the defence structure of Great Britain from 1942 and illustrating the lines of communication and the reporting procedures in relation to the Radio-Location, the RAF, Anti-Aircraft units and other defence and air-raid warning organisations.

Following the new initiative of 1942, women were rapidly absorbed into the ROC despite an initial resistance by the older men.

Also, 1942 saw the introduction of mandatory aircraft recognition testing, with three principal grades, for all members of the ROC.

(if senile old gentlemen can be so described) in the Corps as it is [*sic*]. It is they who we wish to replace.' With the backing of Sir Charles Portal, the Chief of the Air Staff, the writing was on the wall and all ROC activities, including the Club and its Journal were immediately made 'official' and therefore brought under direct Air Ministry control. To bolster ROC morale, which had been considerably weakened by the implementation of these changes, Air Chief Marshal Sir Sholto Douglas, who had replaced Dowding as C-in-C Fighter Command, issued a statement on the value and future of the ROC. In it he praised the work of the Corps during the first three years of the war, emphasising that the ROC and Radio-Location were equal partners in the air-raid reporting system. He concluded by asking all members of the Corps to strive for the highest levels of proficiency and to rise to the new and exacting demands which were being placed on their energy and devotion to duty. Signed Sholto Douglas and dated 21st August 1942, this message was printed on a single sheet of paper and to bolster morale a copy was distributed to every single member of the ROC.

The Report of the Inter-Service Recognition Committee was also taken into account by the Army's AA Command, the Army's Home Defence Forces and the Home Guard. The Army's own paper on the subject of recognition training, that had been submitted to the committee, was masterminded by General Sir Frederick

Pile, C-in-C AA Command, one of the Chiefs of Staff and the main War Office representative on the Inter-Service Recognition Committee. In it he had rapidly drawn the conclusion that the existing recognition school needed both to be expanded and allocated a higher budget. To achieve this the AACRS was reformed on 14 August 1942 into the War Office School of Aircraft Recognition (SAR) and transferred from its then Buckhurst Park base to Albury Hall, near Bishop Stortford in Hertfordshire. Almost at the same time the RAF VART Committee upgraded the Recognition Training Wing to the Central School of Aircraft Recognition (CSAR) and put forward proposals to relocate it from the Isle of Man to a central location in southern England. The Admiralty remained steadfast in its insistence that all of its existing arrangements (which included its Fleet Air Arm pilots being taught basic aircraft recognition techniques during their *ab initio* training with the RAF and aircraft recognition being taught as part of the syllabus at the Gunnery School at HMS *Excellent* in Portsmouth) were quite adequate provided they were regularly supplied with updated material from the MAP. Given the limited spheres of operation of FAA pilots and the many and varied theatres of war in which Royal Navy ships were involved, they were probably correct. This still left the other members of the Inter-Service Recognition Committee somewhat nervous and the RAF continued with its explicit instruction to pilots to keep well clear of Royal Navy vessels.

VOLUME 1   NUMBER 1

AIRCRAFT RECOGNITION

THE INTER-SERVICES JOURNAL

SEPTEMBER 1942

The first copy of the new 'official' inter-service recognition journal.

emphasis firmly on training and techniques. Although it was to be an 'official' publication and only available via official channels, it was to be a low-grade restriction and therefore to be read freely by all those who could gain access to a copy. Gone now were the rigid adherences to mnemonics, such as Mr Saville-Sneath's simple but much criticised 'WET-FUR' (Wings, Engine, Tailplane, Fuselage, Undercarriage, Radiator). Instead, continually evolving techniques for learning were contributed by various instructors responsible for teaching the subject. The relative sizes of different aircraft were presented monthly in a combined silhouette chart and significant differences between two similar types, often one Allied and one enemy, were reinforced in order to stamp out many of the possible dangerous areas of confusion.

With committees begetting committees which beget sub-committees there was, by the autumn of 1942, a formal structure of inter-service command dominated by the Air Ministry. What remained was to fine tune and tidy up the loose ends. The first of these was the production of an inter-service aircraft recognition publication. The decision to produce a monthly journal had been made earlier that year, in June, by the Inter-Service Recognition Committee, with the firm intention of dispensing with the purchasing requirements for *The Aeroplane Spotter* and the ROC Club's *'Journal'*. The new publication, *Aircraft Recognition*, was set to launch in September 1942 under the MAP with an editorial committee of seven headed by Peter Masefield. The brief was to produce a 36-page magazine that contained the best features of all previous recognition publications, but with the

Photography, of a very high standard, was to dominate the publication with silhouettes being restricted to presenting new or revised AP.1480 sheets prior to their distribution. 'Sillographs' (a silhouette form created by blacking-in photographs of aircraft in flight), which had been invented during the previous 18 months and were much in favour with the ROC, were presented as one of the monthly recognition tests.

Using paper of a quality unaffected by normal 'War Standard Economy' restrictions and using a second colour to good effect, the production standard of *Aircraft Recognition* was superior to that of any other recognition or aviation publication although it owed much to its predecessor, *The Journal of the Royal Observer Corps Club*, in both standard and format. And, like its predecessor, it formulated a policy of a practical

114

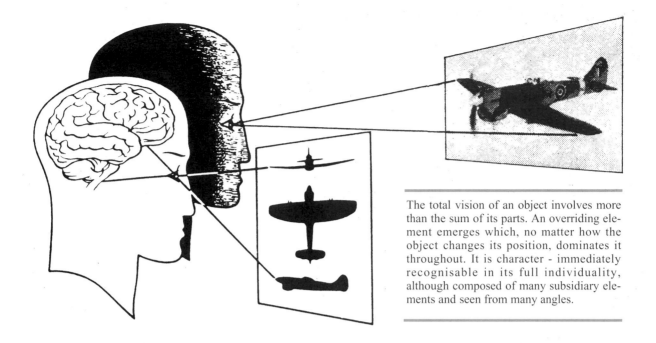

The total vision of an object involves more than the sum of its parts. An overriding element emerges which, no matter how the object changes its position, dominates it throughout. It is character - immediately recognisable in its full individuality, although composed of many subsidiary elements and seen from many angles.

approach to studying aircraft recognition combined with an explicit interest in the aeroplanes themselves. To this end much was made of different approaches to teaching and a series of articles detailed both the working components of various aeroplanes, including the appendages that would add to a silhouette, and the theory of flight itself. Realisation that the study of photographs and silhouettes alone could prove to be an abstract endeavour, great emphasis was placed on getting to know and understand each individual aeroplane. Following the theory 'that

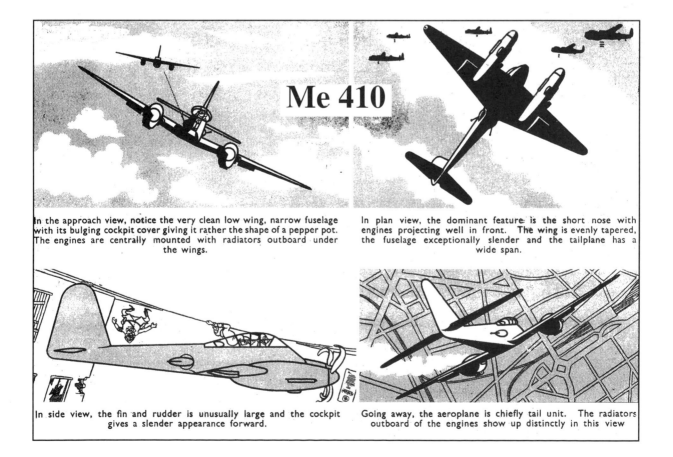

Me 410

In the approach view, notice the very clean low wing, narrow fuselage with its bulging cockpit cover giving it rather the shape of a pepper pot. The engines are centrally mounted with radiators outboard under the wings.

In plan view, the dominant feature is the short nose with engines projecting well in front. The wing is evenly tapered, the fuselage exceptionally slender and the tailplane has a wide span.

In side view, the fin and rudder is unusually large and the cockpit gives a slender appearance forward.

Going away, the aeroplane is chiefly tail unit. The radiators outboard of the engines show up distinctly in this view

115

"AN AIRCRAFT A DAY" — "KEEPS JERRY AT BAY"

SUPERMARINE SPITFIRE IX

MODEL CHANGED DAILY

PLYWOOD OR BAIZE BACKBOARD

WOOD BLOCK, PERMANENTLY FIXED, PAINTED SKY BLUE.

PHOTOS, PRESS CLIPPINGS & DRAWINGS, CHANGED DAILY

to sculpt a figure is to know the person', a great deal of attention was given to the making of model aircraft and to their dramatic presentation and display. Admittedly official MAP silhouette models were by now much more freely available and the handling of them was much encouraged. But, presented as a finished item, these did not allow for the necessary personal input which would lead to an understanding of an aeroplane's

shape. To encourage the doubtful to try their hand, *Aircraft Recognition* published a couple of easy-to-build plans of clever flat-cardboard silhouette models that worked in three dimensions. These were well received and it is interesting to note that the Germans were promoting exactly the same type of models at the same time in order to stimulate aircraft recognition interest among both air crews and anti-aircraft batteries.

Schattenrißmodelle im Flugzeugerkennungsdienst

Von Hauptmann A. Weber, Berlin

Mit Genehmigung des Verlags A. Limbach, Berlin, werden auf dem Bauplan dieses Heftes die Bauzeichnungen für den Nachbau von vier Schattenrißmodellen veröffentlicht. Auf die Bedeutung derartiger Schattenrißmodelle für den Unterricht in der Flugzeugerkennung ist schon in dem Aufsatz des Januarheftes 1942 „Flugzeugerkennung in den Modellfluggruppen", Seite 3, hingewiesen worden.

Abb. 1. Schattenrißmodell „Me 109 F"

Abb. 2. Schattenrißmodell „Ju 88"

Abb. 3. Schattenrißmodell „Vickers Spitfire"

Abb. 4. Schattenrißmodell „Ju 87 B"

A Silhouette Model

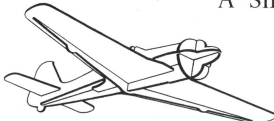
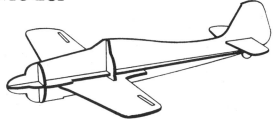

THE FOCKE-WULF FW 190A3

TRACE these diagrams on to cardboard, cut out, and assemble according to instructions.

Obviously the size of the slots will have to be varied according to the thickness of the cardboard used, though for the best results in the scale reproduced the cardboard should be no thicker than indicated on the drawing.

The utmost care must be taken in cutting out the slots and tabs.

ASSEMBLY INSTRUCTIONS

1. Bend wings (A) at the centre line and insert sideways in the fuselage (B) through slot (A1).
2. Take cross-section (C) and insert in slot (C1) of the fuselage and slot (C2) of the wing section.
3. Bend forward the wing supports of (C) so that the tabs slip into the appropriate slots at the extremities of the wings.
4. Insert section (D) in slot (D1) of the fuselage and through slot (D2) of cross-section (C).
5. Insert tailplane (E) in slot (E1) of the fuselage.
6. Insert cross member (F) in slot (F1) of the fuselage.
7. Insert cross member (G) in slot (G1) of the fuselage.

Note : In certain front and rear aspects of the assembled model better results will be achieved by bending section (D) upwards so that it touches the tailplane.

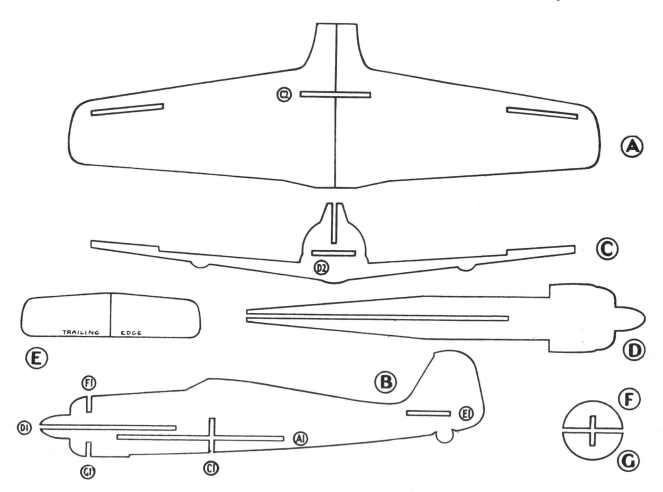

Day to day work in the London, Stratton Street, offices of *Aircraft Recognition* was under the watchful eye of Douglas Jenkins, who effectively acted as editor. It was he who rescued the young Michael Cummings from silhouette draughting duties at Harrogate, having seen some examples of the 'unofficial' caricatures that had found their way onto the department's walls. This followed from the successful use of cartoon drawings in *The Journal of the Royal Observer Corps Club* and also stemmed from a comment made by the Inter-Service Recognition Committee in

Answers on the Acknowledgments page.

There are thirteen aeroplanes, Allied and Enemy, hidden in this scene. Can you find and name them?

118

their Report: 'That lessons should be learnt from the success of the RAF's monthly, *Tee Emm* [home of Anthony Armstrong's 'Pilot Officer Prune'] and from Wren's Oddentifications.' Michael Cummings was, therefore, in addition to his staff artist duties, given a free hand to create a new series of recognition caricatures which he did in a clever composite form using significant elements of different aircraft to create personalities and total drawings with their own scenarios. These were well received and before long *Aircraft Recognition* was also publishing the first of the 'Cummings' cartoons that would lead to a renowned post-war career.

Under the guiding hand of its editorial committee Aircraft Recognition was able to remain flexible to the needs of the three services, the ROC and the defence organisations while maintaining direct links to the Air Ministry and Air and Military Intelligence. Material for publication was either created by the committee or commissioned from an expert, with certain outside contributions submitted for consideration. Notable contributors included Charles Gibb-Smith of the Royal Observer Corps and the Ministry of Information, who had already published his own highly praised book on aircraft recognition - Flt Lieut 'Chris' Wren of the RAF School of Aircraft recognition and *The Aeroplane* - and Sub Lieut Russell Brockbank RNVR who was already an acclaimed cartoonist particularly in the motoring press and who had found himself involved in aircraft recognition. The directors of Temple Press feared that the loss of thousands of copies of *The Aeroplane Spotter* due to the cancellation of

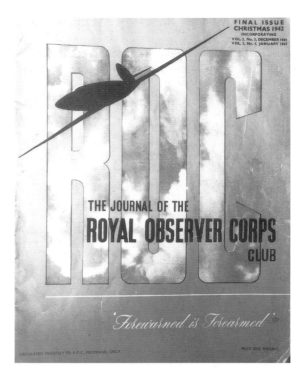

The final issue of the ROC's own Club Journal.

'official' orders would severely dent the publication. Instead Service personnel, accustomed to reading it regularly, now took to buying their own copies and sales were unaffected. *The Royal Observer Corps Club Journal*, however, was doomed and lasted just the few months until December 1942 (determined to close with a bang rather than a whimper the staff put together a special bumper double number which contained a few pages of full colour).

Each of these drawings is made up of the recognition features of an aeroplane. Can you name them?

Answers on the Acknowledgments page.

A Spitfire Mk IX seen from the camera platform of the RAF Benson Photographic Unit's Hudson.

In a final move to fulfil the requirements of the Inter-Service Recognition Committee Report, the question of 'official air-to-air' photographers versus those from the commercial magazines, was solved by seconding certain photographers from *The Aeroplane* and *Flight* to work for the Air Ministry. They were attached to the special

Photographic and Film Unit which was formed at RAF Benson, with a twin-engine, twin-tail, Hudson at its disposal. They were still allowed to continue with their normal work on the magazines, thus giving the Air Ministry the best of both worlds. During early 1943 the 'Flash Recognition Trainer' arrived from the United States for evaluation. This was a projection device with variable shutter speeds up to 1/100th of a second and was used to teach absorption of all the salient features of an aeroplane silhouette, sillograph or photograph without analysing it. Shutter speeds were progressively increased as student proficiency increased with the aim of being able to distinguish in a split second between friend or foe. Specifically introduced for training aircrew, the 'Flash Trainer' was the only significant development in aircraft recognition training to emerge after the dramatic restructuring of 1942.

The two aircraft recognition schools, the War Office SAR and the RAF CSAR, continued to expand. Peter Masefield remained as Editor of *The Aeroplane Spotter* until June 1943 when he was appointed aide to Lord Beaverbrook, Minister of Aircraft Production (but retaining his involvement with *Aircraft Recognition*). By the end of 1943 Britain's defences were well equipped to identify 'the intruder' whether he

In Germany the Luftwaffe used models not only for recognition but also to practise fighter tactics as is seen here with the pilots of a Bf 109 G equipped Geschwader JG4 studying a B-17 Fortress.

came by night or day and, well aware of this, the Germans changed tactics. This time the menace was from 'infiltration' when a single German intruder would attach, in cloud, to the rear of a returning RAF bomber stream thus evading identification by Radio-Location (now termed Radar by agreement with the Americans in order to avoid confusion with their own words for different navigational systems). Transmitted IFF codes were no guarantee since the Germans had acquired MK III sets from downed RAF aircraft and were openly using them to avoid detection particularly in attacks on warships and convoys. Modified procedures with a series of continually changing transmission codes largely solved the maritime problem and returning 'friendly' aircraft were also expected to be transmitting a code set for the operation. Even so, a damaged RAF bomber might well not be able to transmit and it was the role of the Inter-Service Recognition Committee, now it had seemingly successfully dealt with the question of visual aircraft recognition, to address itself to this new and quite difficult problem.

'On the subject of aircraft recognition,
Just remember, as your bullets you send,
That good flying won't lead to perdition,
But good shooting might be at a friend.'

Anthony Armstrong 'Tee Emm' - 1943

END OF AN ERA

Towards the close of 1943 the emphasis of the war against Germany changed from one of defence to the offensive. In Hitler's 'Fortress Europe' the effectiveness of the Luftwaffe was severely reduced and intense Allied bombing raids on Germany had considerably weakened its war economy. The wheel of fortune had also turned in the Soviet Union where, after two years of devastating retreats following the German invasion of June 1941, the massive offensive actions of August-November 1943 now gave the Russians the initiative. With unrelenting pres-

sure, and backed by seemingly unending supplies of men and machines, a valiant Red Army succeeded in recapturing much of the territory occupied by the Germans and in December were back in the old Russian city of Kiev. At the Teheran Conference of the Allied Heads of State, to 'establish military strategy for 1944', Stalin reiterated the Soviet Union's demands for the opening of a Second Front. By this he meant that the First Front was the Soviet-German, which he controlled, and the other Allies should now press forward from Great Britain onto the Continent. The objective, it was unanimously agreed, was now the fall of Berlin and that 1944 would see the establishment of a 'Western'

Front. Although these decisions were not made public, from January 1944 onwards 'invasion fever' mounted in Britain and the questions were no longer 'if' but 'when?' and 'where?'.

The Red Air Force had been the subject of many articles in *Aircraft Recognition* and *The Aeroplane Spotter*, particularly because it had been supplied with Spitfires and Hurricanes by the RAF and had received thousands of aircraft on 'lend-lease' from the Americans. This had nothing to do with the abilities or otherwise of 'Russian' aircraft design or capability but was to supplement the numbers of aircraft that were needed to hold the Germans in place after the Soviet Union had relocated its aircraft factories beyond the Urals. Primarily tactical, the Red Air Force specialised in advanced low-level bombing providing front-line support for troops and tanks. The high-speed 'Russian' fighters were initially used in a defensive role against Luftwaffe bombing and strafing raids, but subsequently created a vital air umbrella for the Red Army's advancing armoured forces. This did not, however, preclude a potential change in Soviet tactics and the study of 'Russian' aircraft gained a certain significance for both the RAF and the Army's AA Command. In an invasion force, both would be expected to recognise these new 'friendlies'

especially when the two Fronts moved closer towards Berlin. At least that was the theory. In truth a deepening mistrust of Stalin's territorial aims was held by the British War Cabinet and the Allied Chiefs of Staff. In their minds there was the possibility of a new enemy who might have to be halted once Germany had surrendered. This placed an urgent responsibility on the Air Ministry to glean as much information on the Red Air Force as possible in order to provide photographs and drawings for recognition training. This was achieved during the early months of 1944, with little or no help from the Soviet Union, up-to-date photographs proving particularly difficult to obtain. Revised AP.1480 silhouette sheets, together with some hastily produced models, were issued with instructions to both the RAF CSAR and the War Office SAR that: 'All known front-line Russian aircraft must now be included in the syllabus.'

The Allied assault on the Continent, codename 'Overlord', required a massive degree of planning all of which had to be conducted in strict secrecy, precise details being kept even from the officers who were in operational command. As a Combined Services operation its overall command had to be absolute, with no question of orders being channelled in the normal manner.

A Yakovlev Yak-3 (the topline Russian fighter) of the 'Normandie-Niemen (Fighter) Regiment' of French volunteers who flew with the Red Air Force on the Third Soviet Front from mid-1944.

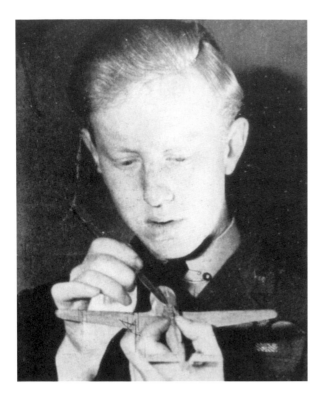

Know your adversary - RAF fighter 'Ace' Ginger Lacey models a Focke-Wulf Fw 190 as did many fighter pilots while awaiting the call to scramble.

Recognise your adversary - regular nissen-hut instruction for spotters attached to anti-aircraft batteries was an essential part of the routine.

Invasion plans had been in existence since 1941 and were continually modified to take account of the changing nature of the war until the creation of COSSAC (Chiefs of Staff to the Supreme Allied Commander) in 1943. It was that plan that General Dwight Eisenhower inherited when he was made Supreme Allied Commander for the invasion and COSSAC was changed to SHAEF (Supreme Headquarters Allied Expeditionary Force) in January 1944. Further modifications to the plan extended the attacking front from 25 to 40 miles of France's Normandy coastline and delayed the date of invasion from May to the first week in June. In essence the plan was simple. Airborne divisions were to be dropped behind the enemy coastal positions in the early hours of the morning, followed by intensive inland bombing raids by the Allied air forces and by extensive Allied naval bombardment of the German coastal defences. Next, a mass amphibious invasion of the beaches to secure the coastal defences while the Allied air forces continued to attack and bomb inland, clearing a path for the Allied armies to advance. All of this would take place under a low-level air umbrella provided by Allied fighters who would relocate to suitable French landing grounds as soon as these could be seized and secured. This plan required some 15,000 sorties to be flown by the Allied air forces, both strategic and tactical, over a sea and land operation which would include some 5,000 vessels (including the landing craft) and some 450,000 troops plus tanks, guns and other fighting vehicles.

With the Luftwaffe expected to make every attempt possible to repel the invading forces, accurate aircraft recognition was high on the priority list for invasion planning, especially since Allied low-level fighters would be vulnerable to 'friendly' small-arms fire. The Inter-Service Recognition Committee, called on to identify particular areas of concern, made two recommendations for visual aircraft recognition which it felt would be vital to the total success of the invasion: 1) A basic system in which all Allied aircraft could be easily recognised by all participating forces, the vast majority of which had no aircraft recognition training; 2) The provision of trained aircraft recognition observers who could identify the correct targets for the initial anti-aircraft fire, the majority of which was expected to be generated by Allied vessels during the actual landings.

The first of these recommendations had a precedent in the earlier problems of the Hawker Typhoon. When finally it became operational as the RAF's new high-speed ground-attack aircraft at the end of May 1942, its particular shape, which in many ways resembled a Focke-Wulf Fw 190, had not been taken into account. The immediate result was that two Typhoons were shot down by No 56 Squadron Spitfires on the second day of operations. After a further five Typhoons had been shot down by 'friendly' fire, and a long list of attacks with less devastating results had been submitted to the Air Ministry, action was taken to apply special markings. These initially comprised bands of yellow encircling each wing in line with the inner cannon. Further 'friendly' attacks proved this was not

the invasion forces during the final briefing.

The second of the Inter-Service Recognition Committee's recommendations touched on an area of long-held concern, namely the ability of the Royal Navy and the Mercantile Marine to recognise visually 'friend' from 'foe'. During the invasion the normal exclusion zone for aircraft around Royal Navy vessels would have to be suspended. In addition the US Navy, which had received no training in aircraft recognition for the European theatre, would be taking part. The ideal solution was to use men from the ROC

The Hawker Typhoon I in the 'white nose and stripes' markings for the mid-1942 'recognition' trials.

enough and markings were changed to four stripes of black interspersed by three large white stripes on the underside of the wings, with an all-white nose. This immediately solved the problem of recognition but made the aircraft too conspicuous to the enemy and the all-white nose was dropped in favour of the normal Fighter Command colours. The success of these recognition markings provided the perfect model for the Allied air forces invasion markings and it was decided to implement a design of three white bands separated by two black bands. This was to encircle the wings (top and underside) and the rear fuselage of all Allied aircraft that were to be used. In practice 'three equal bands of white' were the designated recognition markings. Most of these were hastily applied to the aircraft the day before 'D-Day' and their purpose revealed to

but it was anticipated there would be Admiralty resistance. Especially since the Navy had, over the past year, made a determined effort to drum the importance of accurate aircraft recognition into its Fleet Gunnery Officers, lookouts and gun crews. Another problem was the DEMS (Defensively Equipped Merchant Ships - armed with light anti-aircraft guns) on which aircraft recognition abilities were almost non-existent. Without any prior consultation, the commander of the Allied Expeditionary Air Force (AEAF), Air Chief Marshal Sir Trafford Leigh-Mallory, issued a request on 11th March for some 2,000 ROC observers to be based on Allied ships during the invasion. This was, however, re-reviewed at a SHAEF planning meeting held on 5th of April in which the Admiralty approved 'a requirement' for 'spotters' on all non-Royal

Navy vessels, limiting the number to 240 observers, who would work in pairs. The US Navy, aware of its deficiencies, requested 300 observers to serve as 'Aircraft Identifiers', both instructing and observing for their gun crews. A further problem was the ROC, which although run on military lines and under Air Ministry control, was technically a civilian force. It was therefore decided to enrol each of the ROC observers into the Royal Navy, under a 'Seaborne' scheme, for one month's service (extendable to two) as Petty Officers. They would wear their normal ROC uniforms but with a 'Seaborne' shoulder flash and a 'RN' arm-band. An Air Ministry confidential order, 'Special Scheme for Royal Observer Corps Participation in Forthcoming Operations', was issued on 28th April and resulted in over 1,000 observers volunteering for duty. This was reduced to 796 after medical filtering and by the most stringent of aircraft recognition tests. Further specific aircraft recognition instruction was given to the selected observers, who were mustered at a ROC Depot set up at the Royal Bath Hotel, Bournemouth. By 15th May, over 500 had been drafted to their appointed ships in the convening bases at Cardiff, Plymouth, Southampton and London.

'D-Day' was set for 5th June but, because of low cloud base over the area of operations which would have considerably hindered the tactical air support, it was postponed for 24 hours. On 6th June 1944, 'Overlord' commenced and the land-

Above -'Seaborne Aircraft Identifiers', observers of the Royal Observer Corps (temporarily enrolled as a Petty Officers in the Royal Navy), were essential to the success of 'Overlord'.

Below - An airborne view of the multitude of vessels off the Normandy coast during the invasion.

Coastal Command Warwick Mk Is (successor to the Wellington), with invasion stripes, operated in both General Reconnaissance and ASR roles (note underslung lifeboat) during operation 'Overlord'.

ings followed the strategic bombing as planned with the Allies successfully seizing most of the beachheads. The Germans were either cut-off and contained, or in retreat. In the following days 'Mulberry', a huge artificial harbour of pontoons, and 'Pluto', an undersea oil pipeline, were established to feed yet more tanks, troops and supplies onto the Continent. Although resistance to the invasion was fierce in places, the Germans were largely taken by surprise. They had been deceived into believing the invasion would be in the region of the Pas-de-Calais and had no immediate reinforcements available. During 'D-Day' the AEAF was controlled by Wg Cdr A H D Livock aboard the Royal Navy's headquarters vessel HMS *Bulolo*. He reported: 'The regularity with which large formations of our own aircraft of every type flew over reminded one of Clapham Junction during a Bank Holiday weekend.' Although there were spasmodic attacks on the invasion beaches and shipping by the Luftwaffe, its potential for immediate retaliation had been destroyed by the sheer volume of the Allied air attacks. Nevertheless, there was a great deal of anti-aircraft fire generated by the nervous invading forces. Two of the ROC's 'Seaborne Aircraft Identifiers' reporting on activity in their sector commented on the tendency to open fire on any aircraft which appeared to pose a threat: 'The majority of the gunners in the area were possibly seeing action for the first time and thousands of guns opened fire, whilst noise and lack of communications with the landing craft, which were the chief offenders, added

to the difficulties.' Despite this, the presence of the 'Seaborne' observers was acclaimed a huge success and there were thousands of reports of fire at 'friendly' aircraft being halted due to ROC advice. Even so Allied losses amounted to 118 aircraft during the 24 hours of 'D-Day', the majority of which were directly attributable to anti-aircraft fire.

With supply operations continuing throughout June and the land forces pushing steadily eastward, a need for aircraft recognition specialists to work with the mobile anti-aircraft units became apparent. Suggestions by the British 21st Army Group and the RAF's 2nd Tactical Air Force (2nd TAF) that, 'Following their success during the Normandy landings, the ROC should continue as a landborne force of aircraft identifiers', were discounted. Observer Capt V O Robinson and six ROC officers were, however, dispatched to France to report on the standard of aircraft recognition. They conceded there was an urgent need for instruction but unaccountably their recommendations were not made to the Commandant of the ROC until late September. Meanwhile the War Office SAR had already preempted the situation by training a number of field instructors and equipping them with mobile classrooms to supply updates and refresher courses in aircraft recognition. By the time Paris was liberated on 25th August 1944, the standard of aircraft identification and recognition by the Allied forces, aided by mobile Radar centres and RAF Sector Control, was already rising.

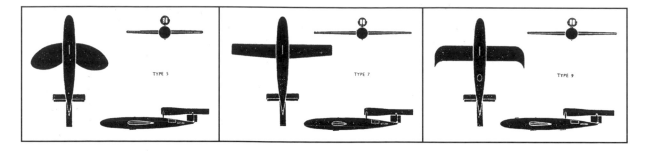

First impressions, drawn by members of the public, of the V-1 'Flying Bomb' which were sent to The Aeroplane Spotter - later intelligence claimed that one of the first V-1s had a tapering wing shape.

While the Allied forces pressed home the Second Front in Normandy, the Germans opened a new offensive strategy which came as no surprise to the Allied Chiefs of Staff but was a tremendous shock for the rest of Britain. The V-1 was a pilotless aircraft controlled by a gyro-driven automatic-pilot linked to a compass and powered by a constant volume pulse-jet fitted to the fuselage and tailplane. Launched from a short ramp, it carried a 1,870 lb high explosive warhead at a maximum speed of 390-410mph with a range of 150 miles. With its pre-set distance achieved small detonators locked the V-1's elevators and deflected small flaps to lower the nose of the bomb. With a change of attitude the engine would cut and it would dive down on a random target, detonating on impact. During the summer of 1943, Military Intelligence became aware of German experimental work on reprisal weapons, which included rocket projectiles and aerial torpedoes, centred at Peenemunde on the Baltic coast. A heavy raid by the RAF during that autumn destroyed part of the complex. But, subsequent reports suggested that work still progressed and responsibility was transferred to Air Ministry Intelligence. In early 1944 WAAF Flt Off C Babington-Smith of the RAF Central Interpretation Unit identified 'a small aircraft-like machine on a ramp' in a reconnaissance photograph taken over the Peenemunde satellite at Zempin. This was a breakthrough and further information from agents, combined with British scientific analyses, proved it to be a pilotless aircraft powered by a constant volume jet. Compiled data allowed AI.2(g) to build a complete profile of the pilotless aircraft including its probable altitude, speed and warhead capacity. Towards the end of April 1944, the revived Air Defence of Great Britain network (ADGB - which included Radar, Fighter Operations, AA Command and the ROC) was informed of Germany's new 'secret' weapon and what to expect in terms of targets and possible numbers of launchings. As a result a crash procedure for 'Diver' (codename from January 1944) was

evolved by the ROC to immediately identify the V-1s and report positions and tracks, overriding all other aircraft movements.

The first 'Flying Bomb' (official name from June 1944) was launched against London on 13th June 1944 and the 'Diver Procedure' immediately initiated by the Observer Post at Dymchurch, Kent. On 15 June, just after dusk, the attack was resumed with 75 V-1s exploding on land followed by 65 the next day. Reports of

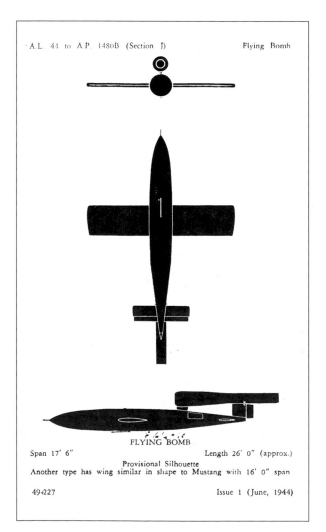

A.L. 44 to A.P. 1480B (Section J)   Flying Bomb

FLYING BOMB

Span 17' 6"   Length 26' 0" (approx.)

Provisional Silhouette
Another type has wing similar in shape to Mustang with 16' 0" span

49-227   Issue 1 (June, 1944)

these raids by members of the public, together with their silhouette impressions of the V-1, were sent to *The Aeroplane Spotter*, and in the absence of any official silhouette were duly published. The Air Ministry silhouette was classified and temporary, awaiting the opportunity to examine a V-1 that failed to detonate. Official reports showed that the 'flying bombs' ran a straight track, usually made landfall between Dover and Brighton, and flew at either '3,000ft and above' or '1,000ft and below'. They were easily recognised by the rasping sound of the pulse engine and a large tail of flame from the rear of the jet. Defence against these attacks was very difficult and never wholly resolved. The first consideration was destruction by anti-aircraft fire and General Sir Frederick Pile, in liaison with the ADGB commander, Air Marshal Sir Roderic Hill, set up a belt of gun emplacements from Beachy Head to Dover some 5,000 yards deep and firing 10,000 yards out to sea. Next, came the use of balloons which could arrest the V-1s in flight and a massive 'Diver Barrage' was erected inland on a line from mid-Surrey to mid- Kent. A final consideration was interception by RAF fighters of which only two, the Spitfire XIV and the Hawker Tempest V, had the necessary speed. This tactic needed very early warning of the V-1s' approach and as long a range as possible. It was therefore decided to position RAF Controllers for 'Diver Operations' at the ROC Horsham and Maidstone centres, with special links direct to the RAF Sectors. Long-range information on high-speed low-flying aircraft proved difficult for existing Radar chains. However, a Microwave Early Warning System (MEWS) developed in America appeared to solve this problem. One of these MEWS installations was already in Britain undergoing evaluation tests prior to its possible operational use in France. This was hurriedly diverted to Fairlight in Sussex and connected to the ROC centres, providing the information required for the RAF fighters to get airborne and into position.

Apart from using cannon fire to destroy the Flying Bombs in mid-Channel, RAF pilots took to 'tucking their wingtips' just under those of the V-1. The effect was to disturb the air pressure and therefore the 'lift' of the V-1's wing thus turning it and upsetting the gyro of its automatic-pilot so the V-1 crashed harmlessly into the sea. This gave rise to the myth that the RAF was 'turning them round and sending them back to fall on the Germans', which was technically impossible but good for public morale. Nevertheless, between 13th June and 5th of September 1944, more than 9,000 V-1s were launched against London and 53 against

'Diver Procedure' in action at No 17 Group Headquarters Royal Observer Corps as the Table Supervisor anticipates a Plotter calling 'Diver Cut' to indicate when a V-1 has started its dive.

Southampton. Of these, over 1,000 malfunctioned after take-off, 3,463 were brought down by the defences, 3,262 made it through but only 2,340 fell on London. Flying Bombs continued to rain on Britain into 1945 but never again with such intensity and in such numbers. RAF action in seeking out and destroying the launch sites met with little success because they were difficult to locate and easy for the Germans to re-establish elsewhere; as the advancing Allied forces began to overrun these sites the Luftwaffe

took to air launching from Heinkel He 111 bombers. This had the advantage of height and enabled Flying Bombs to reach targets as far north as Yorkshire. But, underwing-launching proved difficult with a high level of bomber losses and was given up during January 1945 in favour of a longer-range V-1 launched from sites in Holland. The final phase of V-1 attacks commenced at the beginning of March 1945 and lasted for just four weeks until all the launch sites and the production facilities had been seized by the Allies.

Above - The Wren 'Oddentification' of the Messerschmitt Me 163 'Komet'. Below - Wing Commander Proctor of AI.2(g) studies vulnerability silhouettes of the enemy's new jet aircraft.

In September 1944 Hitler launched his other terror weapon, the V-2 rocket. Propelled by a mixture of liquid oxygen and alcohol it carried a warhead of 1,650 lb and accelerated to a ceiling of 50-60 miles and then descended onto a random target some 200 or more miles distant. Over 1,000 of these deadly missiles struck Britain during a period of seven months, their speed and vertical descent completely defying both Radar and the ROC. The only solution was to destroy the source of V-2 production and their mobile launchers scattered around north-west Europe, creating yet another problem for the Allied armies. What now concerned the Air Ministry was the changing shape and speed of aircraft afforded by the new technology of rocket and jet propulsion. The first rocket-propelled fighter in operation was the tailless Messerschmitt Me 163 'Komet' which had a performance envelope that included a climb rate of over 10,000 feet per minute, a ceiling of 49,000 feet and a top speed of 560mph. It was first flown in May 1944 against the USAAF high-altitude daylight bombers but it was difficult to fly, had an extremely short flight duration (limited fuel capacity) and achieved little success. Germany's jet aircraft programme, which was well in advance of Britain's own work in the field, had produced a partially developed Messerschmitt Me 262 twin-jet engine fighter as early as June 1943. The first production versions were introduced into Luftwaffe units in April 1944, shortly to be followed by the Arado Ar 234 'Blitz', a long-range twin-jet reconnaissance/bomber aircraft. Despite Frank Whittle's experimental work with jet engines early in the war, and a thorough development programme by Gloster, the RAF did not receive its first squadron (No 616) of Meteor III twin-jet fighters until August 1944. And, although designed as a high-speed fighter, the Meteor lacked the manoeuvrability of its best piston engine equivalents, was uneconomic with fuel and no real match for the Me 262 (which became fully operational in October 1944). All of this could have spelled disaster for the invading Allies except that Hitler, who assumed con-

An intact and flyable Me 262 twin-jet fighter (in French markings) captured during the Allied advance.

trol of Luftwaffe policy, insisted on the development of jet aircraft for bombing purposes. Therefore the Me 262, which was an extremely effective high-speed interceptor, was predominantly consigned to a tactical role against the Allied ground forces with its performance impaired by underslung bombs. In this role it was no more nor less effective than other tactical fighters and suffered from air-to-air attacks by the 2nd TAF and the US Army 9th Air Force. Needing longer runways than conventional fighters and also uneconomic with fuel it became prey to the Allied advances during 1945. Starved of suitable airfields and with dwindling fuel supplies its threat rapidly receded.

During the last six months of 1944 the Air Ministry's AI.2(g) strove to obtain as much information as possible on the Luftwaffe's rockets and jets, to produce recognition silhouettes and vulnerability silhouettes which gave 2nd TAF pilots the ideal target zones. By March 1945, with the Allies close to the heart of Germany, orders were given for the production of a new jet fighter for the Luftwaffe. As a 'last ditch stand' the Heinkel He 162 'Volksjaeger' shared some features of the Flying Bomb being small in size with a jet engine mounted on top of the fuselage behind the cockpit. Allocated as a production design in the autumn of 1944, it was specified to fly at 522mph with a ceiling of 39,000 feet and a useful range of some 400 miles. The Air Ministry in London hastily produced drawings based on intelligence information but, by the end of April 1945, only 100 'People's Fighters' had been produced and none had been flown operationally. After a final round of intense pressure by the invading Allied forces, Hitler committed suicide, Berlin collapsed and, realising there was no point in continuing to fight, the German High Command surrendered. By midday on 9th May 1945 the Allies were in control of Germany and all hostilities in Europe had ceased.

The Heinkel He 162 'Volksjaeger' entered Luftwaffe service just in time to be captured by the Allies.

Know Your Friend

HELLCAT

Remember the wing of the HELLCAT (F6F) is low-mid and has a flat centre-section.

MYRT II

JACK II

FRANK I

The HELLCAT'S wing and fin and rudder are square cut.

GEORGE II

HELLCAT

ZEKE 52

OSCAR

JUDY 33

The HELLCAT has a very pronounced humped-back fuselage.

HELLCAT

JILL 12

With the euphoria of Germany's defeat came the order for the ROC to 'stand down' on 12th May 1945. Little public thought was given to the war that continued to rage in the Far East but in the Air Ministry attention was now focused firmly on Japan. The Allied forces of South East Asia Command (SEAC) had been steadily pushing back the Japanese on land as the Americans fought, island by island, across the South Pacific to threaten mainland Japan itself. In the 12th

Mitsubishi A6M5 'Zero-Sen' Naval carrier fighters at Ohita Air Base, Japan in October 1944.

July issue of the *The Aeroplane Spotter* its editor, Charles W Cain, exhorted: 'In Europe all organised fighting has ceased and many people are going back to sleep with the misconception the job is done. THE JOB IS NOT DONE! Over thousands of square miles of ocean and islands in the Pacific a bloody war is being waged against a powerful and desperate enemy. The study of Japanese aircraft recognition is as vital now as the recognition of German aeroplanes was in the past.' In fact Air Intelligence had targeted aircraft of the Japanese Army and Navy since 1938 when the seizure of Southern China had indicated that Japan's aggressive empire-building was more than a distant threat. At that time the first AP.1480(F) silhouettes were produced, albeit based on scant intelligence sent by agents. When Japan entered the war at the end of 1941, the whole subject had to be addressed more seriously and, as had been the case with Germany, great efforts were made by Allied intelligence to obtain the latest details of Japanese operational aircraft. At both the RAF CSAR and the War Office SAR, courses on Japanese aircraft had become part of the curriculum but these were primarily aimed at instructors destined for the Far East. To simplify the recognition of Japanese aircraft, which had unpronounceable names linked to complex numerical sequences, it was decided by the Allies to standardise a nomenclature based on simple male and female forenames. All fighters and floatplanes were given male codenames, all other aircraft were designated female, with transport aircraft given female codenames beginning with the letter 'T'. These names were kept as short as possible for easy use thus: The 'Kawanishi Shiden (Japanese: Violet Lightning) 1-1' fighter became 'George' and the 'Yokosuka Suisei (Japanese: Comet) 3-3' bomber became 'Judy'. The main exceptions to this were training aircraft which were given codenames taken from

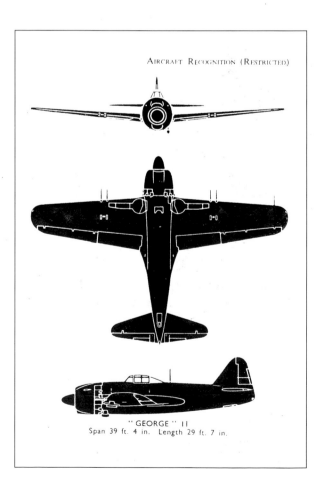

AIRCRAFT RECOGNITION (RESTRICTED)

"GEORGE" II
Span 39 ft. 4 in. Length 29 ft. 7 in.

'Baka', the small Japanese flying bomb flown by suicide pilots of the 'Kamikaze' Special Attack Corps.

flowers, plants and trees. The 'Yokosuka MXY7 Ohka (Japanese: Cherry Blossom)' piloted flying bomb, which was flown by the suicide pilots of the 'Kamikaze (Japanese: Divine Wind) Special Attack Corps', was a further exception being given the ironic Allied codename 'Baka' (Japanese for Fool).

By June 1945 SEAC had all but pushed the Japanese out of Burma and was pursuing a final campaign on a large pocket of Japanese forces who were trying to escape into Siam. The American successes in the Pacific had given the USAAF several advanced strategic bases within bombing range of the Japanese home islands where they had secured a large number of intact Japanese aircraft that had been hastily abandoned. Photographs taken by the USAAF now dominated aircraft recognition training and

Aircraft Recognition, concentrating on Japanese aircraft, became 'Restricted' from June 1945. Politically this was as much an instant method for the MAP to curtail unnecessary production as a need for security, for the content of the journal changed little except for its emphasis. In fact the demand for accurate aircraft recognition now lay almost totally in the Pacific where the US Navy and the USAAF were still heavily under attack from mainland Japan. But the Rising Sun had already started to set. On 6th August 1945, the USAAF dropped the world's first atomic bomb on Hiroshima destroying four square miles of the city and 160,000 people. Three days later a second atomic bomb was dropped on Nagasaki and on 14th August 1945 Japan surrendered unconditionally. The Second World War had come to an end and with it the immediate need for aircraft recognition.

The 'Rising Sun' sets - Mitsubishi K3M 'Pine' and A6M2 'Zero-Sen' with surrender markings.

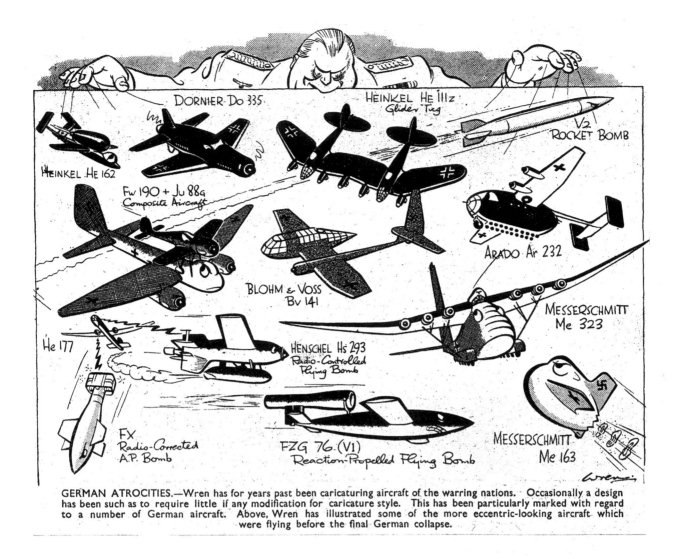

GERMAN ATROCITIES.—Wren has for years past been caricaturing aircraft of the warring nations. Occasionally a design has been such as to require little if any modification for caricature style. This has been particularly marked with regard to a number of German aircraft. Above, Wren has illustrated some of the more eccentric-looking aircraft which were flying before the final German collapse.

The time had now come for an appraisal of what had been achieved. 'VJ Day' (Victory over Japan), although marking the ultimate victory for the Allies, was still remote for most of the people of Britain whose focus remained firmly on the victory in Europe. The Air Ministry, particularly anxious to assess its performance against the Luftwaffe, now had almost unlimited access to examples and variants of German aircraft many of which had been captured in pristine condition or handed over under the terms of surrender. These were taken to the Royal Aircraft Establishment (RAE) at Farnborough for individual examination and evaluation (some floatplanes and one flying-boat were taken to the Marine Aircraft Experimental Establishment at Felixstowe). Some 100 or more examples were variously flown, engine-tested and had their airframes dissected. This was to understand the enemy against which Britain had fought and to determine if there were lessons to be learned, both military and aeronautical, which might be applied to future aircraft production. At the time

of the disbandment of No 1426 (Enemy Aircraft) Flight the RAF Central Fighter Establishment at Tangmere formed a 'Tactics Branch', staffed by ex-wing leaders, to record and evaluate what had been achieved in fighter strategy. Comparisons had to be drawn between the abilities of British and German fighters and tactics tested, accordingly several of the captured aircraft found their way from Farnborough to be flown by some of the illustrious names in Fighter Command.

In June 1945, the MAP together with the Ministry of Information set up a public exhibition, 'Britain's Aircraft', on the bomb site that was once the John Lewis store in Oxford Street. Eleven aircraft were displayed in the relatively confined area, some of them tipped on their side or with wings removed to aid display. The exhibition included Halifax and Lancaster bombers, several of Britain's best aero engines and was staged as a fitting tribute to six years of war production by the British aircraft industry. In mid-September on 'Battle of Britain Day' Londoners were treated to a display of captured enemy aircraft when eight examples were exhibited in Hyde Park and a further two in Trafalgar Square. The big exhibition was yet to come when RAE Farnborough, having completed its principal evaluations, decided to open its doors for an 'Exhibition of German aircraft and Equipment'. This was initially just a static section in a larger air show of the latest British aircraft held on 29th-31st October for VIPs, guests of HM Government, Service personnel and the press. Thirty-three different examples of German aircraft were exhibited and two, the He 162 and the Me 262, were flown to demonstrate performance comparisons between British and German jets. The German aircraft exhibit was again opened to special invitees for the week 4-9th November and, following pressure from the aeronautical press, the public were admitted on Saturday, 10th and Monday, 12th November. This fact was not openly advertised, nevertheless thousands of people flocked to Farnborough to see what they had been up against in the fight for air supremacy. For many, it was the first and only opportunity to see examples of some of these German aircraft at very close range for, immediately the exhibition closed, it was dismantled and most of the exhibits dispersed to be eventually scrapped.

With the September 1945 issue (Vol III No 13) the Inter-Services journal *Aircraft Recognition* suspended production. The RAF CSAR continued but in a much reduced form. The War Office SAR had already moved over to the recognition of tanks, other fighting vehicles and mines. And, the Admiralty was once again primarily concerned with ship recognition. The 'Industrial Raid Spotters' no longer existed and 'officially' aircraft recognition had almost shut up shop and gone home. *The Aeroplane Spotter* (which lasted until July 1948) now remained as the sole survivor of a movement that played a vital part in Britain's defences. However, 'not' forewarned is 'not' forearmed and by March 1946 discussions were taking place in the Air Council about the future needs for an air defence strategy which would include a post-war ROC. In July 1946 a new *Inter-Services 'Aircraft Recognition' Journal*, edited by Flt Lieut 'Chris' Wren and published by HMSO, made its appearance. In an opening statement, Air Vice-Marshal Sir Basil Embry, the Director General of Training for the

Adrian Bishop, an RAE official, at the Exhibition of German Aircraft and Equipment at Farnborough in November 1945, together with Charles W Cain and Gordon Swanborough of The Aeroplane Spotter, behind them is one of the twenty or so piloted V-1 Flying Bombs that were discovered by the Allies.

RAF commented: 'One sometimes hears that with the advent of Radar and the high speeds of the modern aeroplane, that accurate Aircraft Recognition is no longer necessary. I see no foundation for this opinion and, in my judgement, it is vital that we should aim at a far higher standard than we ever did before; for whereas a few years ago, we usually had reasonable time to identify an aeroplane in flight, today high speeds have reduced the time available and tomorrow that time will be still further shortened.' It soon became clear to all concerned that in modern warfare aircraft recognition was only part of the story. By the 1950s, aided by a consensus of opinion that the original defence problems of Identification Friend or Foe with regard to aeroplanes had largely been resolved, *'Aircraft*

Recognition' changed its structure and became the new *Joint Services Recognition Journal* now covering all aspects of recognition 'air-to-air', 'ground-to-air' and 'air-to-ground' and included fighting vehicles and warships. While the RAF CSAR continued (albeit in a reduced capacity) for some years, the ROC was gradually turned into a nuclear warfare warning and radio-active fall-out monitoring organisation linked to the civil defence network and by 1966 had said goodbye to aircraft. History, however, has a habit of repeating itself and with the rationalisation of Britain's forces the need for visual recognition was inevitably lost to the world of electronic aids, only to re-emerge as a practical problem during the Falklands War and as a public forum issue in the recent 'Gulf Conflict'.

'And what did you do in the war, daddy?
I made models and drawings of planes.
And how did that help with the war, laddie?
It showed others they weren't all the same!'

Michael Cummings - 1994

WREN - A TRIBUTE

Ernest Alfred 'Chris' Wren, artist, writer and wit, was perhaps the most original of all the personalities to emerge from the world of aircraft recognition. A student of St Martin's School of Art, he worked as a commercial artist from 1926 to 1939 and, in 1932, joined No 604 Squadron Auxiliary Air Force (AAF) as a rigger and then an armourer. A natural humorist, his affair with aeroplanes continued in earnest when he went to see C G Grey, the Editor of *The Aeroplane*, with a collection of aircraft caricatures. These were duly published and from the mid-1930s Wren became a regular contributor to the magazine. In 1941 the AAF was absorbed into the RAF and Cpl Wren, aided by his association with Peter Masefield, moved to join the new RAF 'aircraft recognition school'. By that time he had started his famous 'Oddentification' series of drawings for *The Aeroplane* and *The Aeroplane Spotter*. These aircraft caricatures were specially drawn so that, aside from the inherent humour, the salient recognition features would be easily remembered. They were often accompanied by one of his 'punning' rhymes to further reinforce the points made in the drawings. A natural instructor, Chris Wren was commissioned in 1943 and made Air Recognition Officer for Combined Operations leading up to the Normandy invasion. In 1946 having left the RAF he became Editor of the revived *Inter-Services 'Aircraft Recognition' Journal* and then Press Relations Officer for the Society of British Aircraft Constructors. Although primarily known for his caricatures of aeroplanes, which continued unabated throughout and long after the war, he also caricatured people which included taking the odd self-effacing look in the mirror. Much loved by all who knew and worked with him, his humour was inexhaustible and his work, which he continued in a freelance capacity, was much in demand. He was still working when he died in 1982 at the annual Empire Test Pilots School 'McKenna Dinner' where, in his own inimitable style, he had always produced a record of the recipients of the awards. Chris Wren was a 'one-off' and whenever aircraft recognition is discussed his name immediately comes to mind.

"The tapered head, the ginger hair,
The outrigged ears, and a prominent pair
Of radial specs, mounted medium high
Through which one can see a watery eye.
A moustache, with anhedral from the roots
Which, though you might not think it suits,
Helps to distiguish from other men,
The characteristic sit of Wren."

The last word from Tony Holland in the pages of The Daily Telegraph on 12th July 1991 commenting on the MoD's annouced intention to disband the ROC.